Faithbuilders Bible Studies

Hosea: The Prophet of the Broken Heart

WIPF & STOCK · Eugene, Oregon

by Mathew Bartlett

Wipf and Stock Publishers
199 W 8th Ave, Suite 3
Eugene, OR 97401

Hosea
The Prophet of the Broken Heart
By Bartlett, Mathew
Copyright©2016 Apostolos
ISBN 13: 978-1-5326-6877-7
Publication date 9/15/2018
Previously published by Apostolos, 2016

Dedicated to all those who are hungry for God's word.

More from Faithbuilders Bible Studies

Faithbuilders Bible studies: Matthew

Faithbuilders Bible studies: Mark

Faithbuilders Bible studies: Ephesians

Esther – Queen of Persia

The Prophecy of Amos – A Warning for Today

Zechariah – Prophet of Messiah

Faithbuilders Bible Studies

The Faithbuilders Bible study series has been developed a useful resource for today's students of God's Word and their busy lifestyles. Pastors, home or study group leaders and indeed for anyone wishing to study the Bible for themselves will benefit from using Faithbuilders studies.

Each volume is the result of many years of group Bible study, and has been revised again and again to be relevant, challenging and faith building whilst remaining clear and easy to understand, helping more people to discover the blessings of God's Word.

Mathew Bartlett holds a Master's Degree in Biblical Studies from the University of Chester, England. Derek Williams is now retired, having been a pastor and preacher for over 40 years.

Contents

Chapter 1:1–11 An Unhappy Marriage 10

    Introduction and Summary 10

    Hosea's Wife and Children 14

Chapter 2:1–23 Marital Problems 19

    Spiritual Adultery 20

    The Restoration of Israel: God's Dealings with People 25

    The Blessings Enjoyed by Believers: A Taste of Things to Come 27

Chapter 3:1–5 God's Love for the Undeserving 30

    Discipline and Restoration for the Erring Nation 32

Chapter 4:1–19 God Goes to Court 35

    The Legal Case Against Israel 35

    Three Sins of Omission 35

    Their Sins of Commission 36

    The Failure of the Priesthood 37

    Turning from God to Follow Demons 39

    A Warning Against Compromise 41

    Israel Provides an Illustration of Apostasy 42

Chapter 5:1–19 Ensnaring the Nation 43

    Ensnaring the Nation 43

Spiritual Bondage 45

Too Late! 46

Sound The Alarm! 47

Destruction of a Nation: but a Remnant Will Return 49

Chapter 6:1–11 A Song of Repentance 51

A Song of Repentance 51

Superficial or True Devotion? 54

Wickedness in the Land 55

Chapter 7:1–16 Spiritual Healing 57

God's Way for Spiritual Healing 57

The Rule of Anarchy 58

Unfaithfulness to God was the Cause of Israel's Weakness 60

Chapter 8:1–14 God's Word Despised 64

Reaping the Consequences 66

A Backslidden People 68

Chapter 9:1–17 Israel's Punishment 70

The Loss of Material Blessings 70

The Loss of Spiritual Blessings 71

The Loss of Children 75

Chapter 10:1–15 Impending Doom 77

    Prosperity Led to Apostasy 77

    Only One Remedy 82

Chapter 11:1–12:1 Israel's Unfaithfulness 85

    God's Unchanging Love 85

    Israel's Slavery 87

    Israel's Future Restoration the Result of God's Love 88

Chapter 12:1–14 Feeding on the Wind 90

Chapter 13:1–16 No Deliverance 96

    Israel's Pride led to its Destruction 96

    No Deliverance from Death 100

Chapter 14:1–9 The Promise of Future Hope 102

Chapter 1:1–11 An Unhappy Marriage

Introduction and Summary

1:1 This is the word of the LORD which was revealed to Hosea son of Beeri during the time when Uzziah, Jotham, Ahaz, and Hezekiah ruled Judah, and during the time when Jeroboam son of Joash ruled Israel.

The prophetic ministry of Hosea can be dated between 760 to 721 BCE, during the reigns of the kings mentioned here.[1] As such he was a contemporary of both Amos, Micah, and Isaiah. The period was one of material prosperity and military/political success, but unfortunately this was not matched by the religious devotion or thankfulness of the people to God. On the contrary, the spiritual condition of the people grew increasingly worse.

When Jeroboam I led the ten tribes to separate from Israel in 930 BCE, he set up golden calves in Bethel and Dan to discourage Israel from crossing over to Judah to worship Yahweh (see 1 Kgs 12). Initially this worship was syncretism—which is to say that the calves were supposed to represent Yahweh, and the worship offered was purported to still be offered in his name. An alternative priesthood set up to facilitate worship separate from the Levites who had remained faithful to Judah. It is imperative to remember that God had instituted the Levitical priesthood and the temple sacrifices etc. whilst Jeroboam's alternative was man-made. Hence the religion proposed by Jeroboam soon degenerated into open idolatry. Hosea

---

[1] Biblical references to the kings of Judah: Uzziah (2 Chron 26:3); Jotham (2 Kgs 15:7); Ahaz (2 Kgs 15:38); Hezekiah (2 Kgs 16:20) and the reign of Jeroboam (II) son of Joash king of Israel (2 Kgs 13:13). Scholars suppose that the dating being given in terms of the kings of Judah rather than those of Israel represents the fact that a later Judean editor was preserving Hosea's prophecies. J. Dearman, The Book of Hosea, NIV Commentary (Grand Rapids: Eerdmans, 2010), 79.

mainly rebuked the practise of Baal worship, which was prevalent at that time. This "god" Baal, had found a powerful advocate in Jezebel, the wife of Ahab (1 Kgs 16:31, 18:4, 19:2, 21:25), and although Jehu had made some attempt to destroy the worship of Baal (2 Kgs 10:28), it was never completely expunged and consequently was revived following his death. God, foreseeing the nation's apostasy, had promised Jehu that his descendants would only reign for four generations;[2] indeed, such was the wickedness of Zechariah that his reign lasted a mere six months.[3] This unfaithfulness to God led ultimately to the exile of the northern kingdom at which point Hosea's ministry appears to have ended.

Baal worship was a primitive kind of nature worship. The word Baal 'master/lord' was a generic word for god, although over time it became primarily associated with the god of storm and fertility—also known as "Hadad"— who was regarded as chief among a panoply of gods. Tatford explains that the worship of Baal involved not only the offering of sacrifices (human and animal) but also acts of so-called "sacred prostitution."[4] Alongside Baal was his female consort Astarte or Ashtoreth, who was depicted as a naked woman riding a lion with a lily in one hand and a serpent in the other. Equally a goddess of fertility, she too was worshipped by sacrifice and sacred prostitution.

The shrines of these gods would have stone pillars (for Baal) and wooden poles (for Ashtoreth), both sexual symbols which symbolised fertility; spaces were set aside for sacred sexual rites, with female prostitutes available for worshippers of Baal and male prostitutes for worshippers of Ashtoreth.[5]

---

[2] 2 Kgs 10:30.
[3] 2 Kgs 15:8.
[4] Frederick Tatford, *Prophet of a Broken Home* (Eastbourne: Prophetic Witness, 1974), 12
[5] See Dearman, 166.

In an agrarian society, fertility of crops meant the difference between life and death, and a woman's fertility was also important, as children were needed to provide for the family. An important aspect of Hosea's ministry involved a reaffirmation that all the good gifts which Israel received were actually the generous gifts of Yahweh and not of Baal. They were using these gifts to make sacrifices for Baal, which God describes as a kind of unfaithfulness akin to adultery. One can readily see why God would choose this imagery in light of the fact that the people had sacralised adultery in their heathen worship.

God had brought Israel to himself in a covenant which the Old Testament describes as being like a marriage (Jer 3:14). Israel, the bride of Yahweh, was to be faithfully devoted to her God, who had commanded "you shall have no other gods" (Exod 34:14). The worship of other gods is therefore described as adultery, and such marital language accentuates the difference between the conduct of a man and wife (Heb 13:4) as followed by the worshippers of Yahweh and the immoral sex rites of the pagans which Israel had adopted. Both Old and New Testaments link idolatry and unfaithfulness to God with an increase in sexual immorality and promiscuity (Acts 15:20; Rev 2:14), and it could be argued that a general departure from God has led to the rise in immorality in modern society.

This makes God's choice of mission for Hosea all the more pertinent. He was instructed by God, despite it being contrary to the law,[6] to take a wife, Gomer, who was known to be sexually promiscuous. Hosea's heartbreaking experience of her unfaithfulness and betrayal was used by God as an object lesson to mirror his own relationship with his people. Both Gomer and Israel were loved, but the more they were loved the more they went astray. Ultimately they were to reap the fruit of what they had sowed. Today, we must also remember that this is a spiritual law (Gal 6:7–8); the believer should value the grace of God and not take it for granted.

---

[6] Deut 22:13–21.

Interestingly the illegitimate children of Gomer are given heart-breaking names about rejection, but they are not rejected by God. This is in accordance with God's mercy and justice, for the sin which led to their illegitimacy was Gomer's not theirs. Hosea cares for and brings them up, just as the wronged God had not neglected to provide for his people. A promise of restoration is given to those who are "not mine." The nation which was God's possession could only be described in this way—an early hint of the divorce formula alluded to in 2:2—only because they had ruptured the covenant of the law. Even so, God's promise of restoration indicates that although Israel may have walked out on God, God had kindly left the door open.

Before we think that God's call to Hosea was unusual, it is worth recalling that prophets were often called to act out their message (e.g. Jeremiah's belt in Jer 13 and Ezekiel's siege in Ezek 4:3). In Hosea's case it was a call to be married to an unfaithful wife, and experience the years of tribulation which this brought him, in order to demonstrate God's sorrow at the way he had been treated by Israel.

One detail of this prophecy which is often overlooked is whether the fate of Israel was shared by Gomer. Israel was unrepentant and so was sent into permanent exile, with many of her citizens killed. Does the analogy work both ways? Was the unrepentant adulteress free from retribution whilst the unrepentant nation died—or did she perish in the Assyrian invasion?

Whilst the picture of Hosea's patient treatment of Gomer is meant to describe God's longsuffering with his people, it does not represent God's attitude toward adultery. In the New Testament adulterers are warned "The Lord will judge" (1 Thess 4:3-6; Heb 13:4). This warning was, of course, written to Christians, and indeed Jesus discussed the matter with his disciples, on several occasions saying that to look at a woman (or man) lustfully—or with sensual thoughts and desires—is adultery in the heart. Jas 1:5 warns that the lust in the heart is what leads to the deed which results in death. We have been warned.

Hosea's Wife and Children

> *1:2 When the LORD first spoke through Hosea, he said to him, "Go marry a prostitute who will bear illegitimate children conceived through prostitution, because the nation continually commits spiritual prostitution by turning away from the LORD."*

The reason for this unusual command of God—that Hosea should marry a prostitute who would be unfaithful to him—is made clear from the beginning—Hosea's marriage is intended to mirror the relationship between God and his people, whom God accuses of whoredom, that is to say unfaithfulness to the covenant.

> *1:3-5 So Hosea married Gomer, the daughter of Diblaim. Then she conceived and gave birth to a son for him. Then the LORD said to Hosea, "Name him 'Jezreel,' because in a little while I will punish the dynasty of Jehu on account of the bloodshed in the valley of Jezreel, and I will put an end to the kingdom of Israel. At that time, I will destroy the military power of Israel in the valley of Jezreel."*

At this early stage in their marriage there is no suggestion of marital difficulties. When Hosea took Gomer she conceived and bore *him* a son. It is not unusual for God to speak about the overall outcome of the prophet's ministry at the beginning of a prophetic book. This is seen in the name given to the first child born; God names the child "Jezreel." The name means "God sows" or "God scatters" (that is, to sow with seed); the plains of Jezreel earned this name by being a fruitful valley for crops. The play on words may begin as a reference to the fact that the boy was truly Hosea's son—his own seed. Yet the way in which God speaks of the nation whom he had sown (an allusion in the sense of begetting them as his children), Israel, indicates that they in turn would reap what they had sowed. The harvest it would reap for sowing iniquity and idolatry would be the end of the kingdom. Here is a further reference to the "scattering" of the people by God through his instrument Samaria. With both of these illusions in mind ultimately the military might of Israel would be broken; that is, utterly defeated in war.

At the same time God is linking the evil behaviour of the people with the behaviour of Jehu, who had gone beyond the divine remit and massacred many in Jezreel. It would be fitting, then, if those who followed his example of disobedience met with disaster in the place where the crime was committed.

However, with the words "I will put an end to the kingdom of Israel" God effectively predicts the outcome of Hosea's ministry—that it would fail to bring the people to repentance.

However, the Lord returns to this same play on words at the end of the chapter. A feature of Hosea (as it is with Isaiah) is that despite the present bleak situation, an idyllic eschatological future is promised.

> *1:6–7 She conceived again and gave birth to a daughter. Then the LORD said to him, "Name her 'No Pity' (Lo-Ruhamah) because I will no longer have pity on the nation of Israel. For I will certainly not forgive their guilt. But I will have pity on the nation of Judah. I will deliver them by the LORD their God; I will not deliver them by the warrior's bow, by sword, by military victory, by chariot horses, or by chariots."*

The text is not clear on the issue, but if we accept from the tone of the verse that the child born to Gomer on this occasion is not Hosea's, then by calling the child "No Pity" God might be reflecting on the fact that Hosea, knowing the child was not his, would have felt no paternal instinct for her. In the same way, despite Israel being his people, they had made themselves illegitimate by their unfaithfulness, and so God will from now show them no more mercy. There will be no forgiveness, for God's plea for repentance would remain unanswered. Their doom at the hands of Assyria was sealed.

In Judah, however, the situation was different. Largely due to the reforms of good kings such as Josiah and Hezekiah, the people of Judah had in a large part turned back to Yahweh. The deliverance mentioned here is probably a reference to the occasion of Senecherib's assault on Jerusalem in the days of Hezekiah. Having defeated the northern kingdom, the Assyrians thought themselves invincible, even challenging Judah's God. But when Hezekiah prayed, the Lord sent an angel to destroy 185,000 enemy troops as they besieged the city, so that the army fled back to Assyria (see Isa 36–37).

> *1:8–9 When she had weaned 'No Pity' (Lo-Ruhamah) she conceived again and gave birth to another son. Then the LORD said: "Name him 'Not My People' (Lo-Ammi), because you are not my people and I am not your God."*

In this case the matter is clearer—the child is almost certainly not Hosea's as he is named "Not My People." The thing is with Israel of course is that they *were* God's people; God's shocking pronouncement indicates just how far they had fallen, to be in breach of the covenant to such an extent that they were considered to be equivalent to the Gentiles—heathen—not my people.

Since they had become like those nations who worshipped idols and not God, God disowns them in a move that might readily be compared to a divorce. Indeed, the words employed "I am not your God" are reminiscent of Israel's divorce practices. This is important as it links into the opening of chapter two, where once again the language of divorce is used.

> *1:10 However, in the future the number of the people of Israel will be like the sand of the sea which can be neither measured nor numbered. Although it was said to them, "You are not my people," it will be said to them, "You are children of the living God!"*

Despite this language and the painful message of the prophet about the punishment of God coming upon an entire generation, God would not forget nor renege on his promise to Abraham (Gen 15:5) that his descendants would be without number. This indicates God's purpose will stand despite the unfaithfulness of his people. An eschatological hope is introduced of the restoration of Israel to the description "children of the living God."

The way the New Testament writers utilise this verse is very interesting. Peter alludes to the idea of those who were once not counted as God's people being included in that group. He writes to believers some of whom were Gentiles that although "you had once not been a people, now you are the people of God. Once you had not received mercy (a reference to the girl's name, and another clear allusion to this chapter) they had now received mercy" (1 Pet 2:10). Peter's reasoning is fascinating; he appears to examine a passage which deals with an apostate Jewish nation being restored to God. Thus in effect he is saying, "if those Jews who, although they were God's people, had so become like the heathen that they are described as 'not my people' and yet could be restored in Christ, then surely those people from the Gentile nations who are called by Christ can be made recipients of the same mercy."

Similarly, Paul takes this verse about Israel's ultimate restoration despite their present alienation and applies it to the situation in which he found himself. In Paul's day, many Jews had rejected Christ and were outside of the new covenant which God had promised. Yet Hosea's prophecy allows Paul to argue that Israel's rejection by God is not permanent, but that once again a restoration may be expected. This hope of Israel's national restoration begins with the call of the Gentile nations to be included in a renewed people of God and culminates with Israel being readmitted to the family of grace. Hence in the writings of both Peter and Paul, Hosea's prophecy foreshadows the way in which the mercy of God has become available to all people through Jesus Christ.

1:11 Then the people of Judah and the people of Israel will be gathered together. They will appoint for themselves one leader, and will flourish in the land. Certainly, the day of Jezreel will be great!

The return of Judah to Jerusalem following the exile may be thought of as a partial fulfilment of these verses, but only if it can be shown that members of the tribes other than Judah, Levi, and Benjamin returned at that time. If such is the case, then Zerubbabel, who led the people at that time (Hag 2:21) may be regarded as the "one leader" spoken of here. Notice how God introduces again this play on words concerning Jezreel—the Lord shall sow or plant—which indicates that God would again plant Israel in the land of Judah. Yet this reunion of the people of Judah and Israel is yet to be fully realised. The leader whom God appoints over his people is the son of David, the messianic ruler who unites the people of God. Since the return from exile there have been many who have fulfilled the role of leader over God's people, but it will be Jesus Christ who rules forever over the united people of God made up of faithful Jews, previously apostate Jews and converted Gentiles—all of whom have been the recipients of God's mercy; and of this kingdom shall there be no end (Isa 9:7; Luke 1:32–33).

Chapter 2:1–23 Marital Problems

Hosea's wife Gomer had been guilty of adultery. As I have suggested two of her children were not Hosea's children. The law allowed a husband in Hosea's situation to divorce his wife. Whilst the legal punishment for adultery was death (Lev 20:10), the custom in some Middle Eastern nations was to strip the woman of her clothes (Ezek 16:39) and expel her from the home.

The words used in verse one were the legal formula for divorce. The law gave Hosea every right to withdraw his support for Gomer and no longer be her husband. A more detailed examination of the passage will reveal that Hosea still loved his wife and wished, under the right conditions, for her to be reconciled to him. The condition was, that she would stop having affairs with other men. If she repented and returned home, Hosea was willing for the relationship to continue. If not, he would disown her she would no longer receive Hosea's support and shelter and would no longer be his wife—this is divorce.

If Gomer did indeed leave her husband's home and stayed with lovers who were unwilling or unable to support her, then she may have begun to realise that life with Hosea was much better. It is therefore possible to imagine her returning, not actually repentant, but merely looking for the benefits that she had once received from her husband. I further suggest that as Hosea received her back, he hoped that she would one day put away her adulterous lovers and be from then forward faithful to him.

It must be remembered that much of the intricacies of the relationship between Hosea and Gomer are conjecture. Whilst these thoughts are applied by the prophet to the situation concerning Israel, I suggest that it is very probable that events between Hosea and Gomer followed such a course. Yet whilst we have applied these words to Hosea and Gomer, they actually relate more fully to God's relationship with his people.

Spiritual Adultery

> *2:1-2 Then you will call your brother, "My People" (Ammi)! You will call your sister, "Pity" (Ruhamah)! Plead earnestly with your mother (for she is not my wife, and I am not her husband), so that she might put an end to her adulterous lifestyle, and turn away from her sexually immoral behavior.*

God accused Israel of committing spiritual adultery; the idolatrous practices of the Israelites bore witness to this (e.g. Jer 3:9; Ezek 16:17). To understand what is meant by "spiritual" adultery we must consider what is involved in physical adultery. Adultery is of course a physical act, because it involves a married man or woman having sexual intercourse with someone other than their own marriage partner. Yet there is more to it than that; the physical act is not isolated from the emotional situation. Adultery happens when someone leaves their first love, preferring the love of another. This gives us a clearer insight into what "spiritual" adultery really is. It is turning from God to love anyone or anything else. In the New Testament, James calls those "adulterers" who prefer the love of the world to the love of God (Jas 4:4).

> *2:3 Otherwise, I will strip her naked, and expose her like she was when she was born. I will turn her land into a wilderness and make her country a parched land, so that I might kill her with thirst.*

We have already mentioned that verse one contains the words of the Hebrew divorce formula. We have also said that the law allowed a husband to divorce his unfaithful wife. Although God's intention for Israel was reconciliation, not divorce and separation, she needed to realise that she could not at the same time be his *and* worship Baal. No one can serve two masters (Matt 6:24). God was quite within his right to say that he would no longer be a husband to Israel. Yet if only the nation would repent, reject the Baalim, return to God, and be pure in their love and devotion to him, then restoration was still possible. If, on the other hand, there was no repentance and change then God, like a jealous husband, would strip his guilty wife naked.

This was a metaphor, of course. Up until that time God had been like a husband to Israel by providing for the nation, feeding and clothing her. He gave her wool and flax to make clothing, and so on—but now these blessings would be denied.

God would remind Israel of the time when their relationship began and the nation was born. This was at the time when God brought them out of slavery in Egypt and made them his own people. Before that there had been no such nation as Israel. Because of their sin, they would again become slaves, this time to the Assyrians. The land would suffer destruction and drought of a kind that would spell death to its inhabitants. This was a very appropriate punishment, since Baal was supposed to be the god of rain and fertility. When God withheld the rain and the crops no longer grew, then Israel would realise how futile it was to serve those gods which are in fact no gods at all.

> *2:4 I will have no pity on her children, because they are children conceived in adultery.*

Just as Gomer's children were not Hosea's but the result of her adulterous union, so the Israelites could no longer be regarded as God's children because of their spiritual adultery. They were, metaphorically, the result of the union between Israel and Baal, and so could no longer expect to be shown the compassion afforded to God's own children.

> *2:5 For their mother has committed adultery; she who conceived them has acted shamefully. For she said, "I will seek out my lovers; they are the ones who give me my bread and my water, my wool, my flax, my olive oil, and my wine.*

The people had adopted the pagan worship of the Canaanites whose land they had possessed, and whom they had failed to drive out fully after

Joshua. They believed that all the good gifts they had (food, water, clothing etc.) were given to them by the idol gods that they worshipped rather than by the true God. In the New Testament James reminds us that every good and perfect gift comes from God (Jas 1:17). They would all be punished for this. As Tatford points out that it was not just the nation as a whole that would suffer punishment, but every individual worshipper of Baal within the nation.[7]

> *2:6-7 Therefore, I will soon fence her in with thorns; I will wall her in so that she cannot find her way. Then she will pursue her lovers, but she will not catch them; she will seek them, but she will not find them. Then she will say, "I will go back to my husband, because I was better off then than I am now."*

God's purpose in all of his actions was to win Israel back to himself. God is always willing to forgive when there is genuine repentance. If Israel would eagerly seek Baalim then God would put everything in their way to prevent them. In other words, when judgment came, the Baalim would not be of any use to them. The people might pray, but God would see to it that no relief was found, lest the people should think that Baal had answered them. Let them pray as much as they wish, no answer would come. The people of Israel should have already learned this lesson from the time of Elijah's challenge on Mount Carmel. No Baalim could help Israel in their time of distress. It is the Lord who both gives benefits and who brings calamity (1 Kgs 18:19–40).

Unfortunately, Israel's return was to be superficial. Rather than being ashamed of the wrong they had done, they merely realised that they were better off materially when the Lord was their God, and so returned to him in order to once again obtain the prosperity and material blessing that they longed for. This is not true repentance.

---

[7] Tatford, 32

> *2:8–9 Yet until now she has refused to acknowledge that I was the one who gave her the grain, the new wine, and the olive oil; and that it was I who lavished on her the silver and gold— which they used in worshiping Baal! Therefore, I will take back my grain during the harvest time and my new wine when it ripens; I will take away my wool and my flax which I had provided in order to clothe her.*

It is difficult for us to understand the full implications of the words, "she has refused to acknowledge" (or "she did not know" in AV). God had brought the Israelites out of Egypt and given them his law. They had the words of the Torah and of the prophets. Surely they could not have been ignorant of all that God had done for them? Yet perhaps ignorance had arisen in Israel due to a neglecting of God's word, which may not have been read as regularly and widely as it should have been. Consider that if men and women today are to find hope and eternal life in Jesus Christ then the word of God must first be made known to them (Rom 10:14).

It is more likely, however, that although the people had heard the words of Moses and the prophets they did not believe them. They "refused to acknowledge" God because their hearts were blinded by unbelief. Hosea lived during a time of great national prosperity, yet the people did not give thanks to God for the gifts that they enjoyed. In fact, they "added insult to injury" by using these gifts to worship their supposed benefactors, the Baalim.

As a result, God was to remove his blessings and his gifts. We can imagine Gomer making presents to her lovers of what Hosea had provided for her. Her husband would be quite right to refuse to provide for her any more if all he gave was only to be given to others. Why should God subsidize the nation's idolatry? He will relinquish responsibility for this unfaithful wife and withdraw his gifts, leaving her naked and destitute.

> *2:10 Soon I will expose her lewd nakedness in front of her lovers, and no one will be able to rescue her from me!*

Still using the imagery of an adulterous wife, God says that when Israel is "stripped of her clothes and sent away" it will be obvious to all that her affection for Baal was misplaced; since neither Baal nor anyone else could save her from his hand.

> *2:11–13 I will put an end to all her celebration: her annual religious festivals, monthly new moon celebrations, and weekly Sabbath festivities—all her appointed festivals. I will destroy her vines and fig trees, about which she said, "These are my wages for prostitution that my lovers gave to me!" I will turn her cultivated vines and fig trees into an uncultivated thicket, so that wild animals will devour them. "I will punish her for the festival days when she burned incense to the Baal idols; she adorned herself with earrings and jewellery, and went after her lovers, but she forgot me!" says the LORD.*

Israel had been given several feasts as joyous occasions for the worship and service of God; but Israel had polluted these feasts, changing them into pagan festivals sacred to the Baalim. God was left out of national life, and so God would put an end to the feast days, since their significance had been lost to the people.

Moreover, further judgments are pronounced against Israel for her unfaithfulness, including that her cultivated fruit orchards and vineyards would return to their wild state. By implication, this meant there were not enough people left alive to tend the fields. It would be for the same reason that the number of wild beasts would increase. This prophecy foretells the forced depopulation of Israel by the Assyrians. The punishment would be severe because she had forgotten God and burned incense to idols. The adorning of oneself with jewels is a reference to the sexual practices of the cult, and to the temple prostitutes, who as we have mentioned before in chapter one, offered sex as a means of worship to the god Baal.

The Restoration of Israel: God's Dealings with People

> *2:14–15 However, in the future I will allure her; I will lead her back into the wilderness, and speak tenderly to her. From there I will give back her vineyards to her, and turn the "Valley of Trouble" into an "Opportunity for Hope." There she will sing as she did when she was young, when she came up from the land of Egypt.*

Once he had stripped her of all her finery, God would seek to win Israel, his "wayward wife", back to himself. It is possible that the wilderness spoken of is the place to which God will scatter the people, or it may indicate a return to their own land which had become a wilderness in their absence.

The word "allure" can mean to appeal irresistibly, constraining to the point of overwhelming all resistance. This is what Christ does to our hearts as he woos us to receive him as Saviour. It is what God will one day do again to the nation of Israel, and perhaps (as many contemporary Christians believe) it may be a future day when Israel will respond to and receive Christ as saviour en mass to which this scripture refers (such a view may be inferred from Rom 11:25–26, where Israel is said to be saved in the eschatological future, after the fullness of the Gentiles has come in).

At that time, he would "speak tenderly to her" as in Isa 40:2, "Speak ye comfortably to Jerusalem, and cry unto her, that her warfare is accomplished, that her iniquity is pardoned: for she hath received of the LORD'S hand double for all her sins."

Similarly, the Holy Spirit speaks to the hearts of all believers, bearing witness to us that we are forgiven, and have become God's children (Rom 8:16).

Tatford says "in the coming exile, he would teach her afresh his love and induce her dependence upon him as he did after her exodus from Egypt.

She could never reform herself unaided and his discipline of her was intended to be educational: it was for the purpose of bringing her back to himself."[8] Hosea's prophecy made clear that although God had given the land of Israel over to the enemy, it would not remain theirs forever. One day God would give his people the land again. What is more, they would be restored in their relationship to him.

God would make the valley of Achor a door of hope. After the defeat of Jericho, trouble came upon Israel because of a man named Achan, who had sinned by disobeying God's command. This caused Israel to be defeated before their enemies at Ai. However, after the valley of Achor, once the sin had been dealt with (Achan and all his family were stoned to death!) Israel went on to victory. The meaning of Hosea's words would have been plainly understood. Only when sin is confessed and put away can fellowship with God be restored.

This verse has a deep significance for every believer. At Achor, sin was dealt with so that Israel might be restored in fellowship with God; whilst at Calvary, God's only Son Jesus took the punishment for the sins of all humanity, dying so that whoever believes in him may be reconciled to God forever. Christ's own valley of Achor was endured on the cross, and his cross has become a door of hope, an entrance to everlasting life (John 10:9; 2 Thess 2:16).

When the time came for Israel to be restored, she would respond to God as she did when she first came out of Egypt—with godly fear, rejoicing, and singing (Exod 14:31; 15:1). In a similar way I believe that a future day is coming when the remnant of Israel will rejoice when they receive Christ as their Saviour. Even now, all who experience salvation, Jew and Gentile alike, "rejoice with exceeding great joy!" (1 Pet 1:8).

---

[8] Tatford, 39

> *2:16–17 "At that time," declares the LORD, "you will call, 'My husband'; you will never again call me, 'My master.' For I will remove the names of the Baal idols from your lips, so that you will never again utter their names!"*

God promise that when he cleanses the hearts of the people of Israel he would also cleanse their lips. No more would the people call God "Baali"; a name which had pagan connotations. Observe that so complete is the power of God to deliver that the result is a complete severing from the old way of life. From now on Israel would call God "Ishi" (meaning "my husband"), denoting an intimate and personal relationship. So complete would be the change that Israel would never again so much as mention the practice of Baal. It would be completely expunged from the land.

Whenever someone comes to know the Lord Jesus Christ as Saviour, the power of sin is broken. Those who once were bound by paganism or witchcraft or any other evil thing break completely free from their old life. This is a very necessary part of the salvation experience. The former life of sin is abandoned (Acts 19:19; 2 Cor 5:17), because Jesus Christ sets us completely free (John 8:36).

The Blessings Enjoyed by Believers: A Taste of Things to Come

> *2:18 "At that time I will make a covenant for them with the wild animals, the birds of the air, and the creatures that crawl on the ground. I will abolish the warrior's bow and sword—that is, every weapon of warfare—from the land, and I will allow them to live securely."*

The result of God's new covenant with his people would be peace forever. Not even the animals would hurt or destroy; weapons are to be banished forever. Whilst believers know and enjoy peace with God now, a day is coming when this peace shall break into time in a way that shall bring a literal fulfilment of this prophecy upon earth. Jesus is our peace, and when he comes to reign on earth for a thousand years, peace will be the foundation of his government (Isa 11:6–9).

2:19 I will commit myself to you forever; I will commit myself to you in righteousness and justice, in steadfast love and tender compassion.

Following Israel's repentance, God would again betroth Israel to himself. This may be how Hosea dealt with Gomer. After he had confronted her about her sin and imposed certain conditions on her she may have repented, and he was willing to take her back as his wife again.

This is what God was prepared to do for his repentant people. They had forsaken him, but when they returned he would be willing to receive them. In a similar way, Christ refuses none who come to him (John 6:37), and in Christ, those who were far off have been brought near to God (Eph 2:13).

In those days, when a girl was betrothed a bride price was paid for her. The price paid by Christ to redeem his bride was his own life. Because of his sacrifice we have entered into a new and living relationship with God, a close and permanent bond. God has taken us for himself in righteousness and justice, for our sin has been dealt with on the cross so that God might have legal grounds for forgiving us (Rom 3:26; 1 John 1:9).

Christ's death commends his love to us (Rom 5:8) and in loving kindness and compassion God has made us his own. Furthermore, he has made us his own in faithfulness, for he will keep his word of promise. In bringing us to himself, God has given us the privilege of being his sons, and so we know the Lord, not with an intellectual knowledge, but with a spiritual understanding—the intimate acquaintance of a son with a father.

2:21–23 "At that time, I will willingly respond," declares the LORD. "I will respond to the sky, and the sky will respond to the ground; then the ground will respond to the grain, the new wine, and the olive oil; and they will respond to 'God Plants' (Jezreel)! Then I will plant her as my own in the land. I will have pity on 'No Pity' (Lo-Ruhamah). I will say to 'Not My People' (Lo-Ammi), 'You are my people!' And he will say, 'You are my God!'"

Although God had promised to punish Israel for her sins by withholding rain and therefore food, new wine, and oil, he promises later to restore his blessings through this poetic picture. The prophet views the heavens crying out to God to allow them to rain and bring blessing on his restored people. The earth also cries out for rain to bring a harvest of blessing for the redeemed. God says that he will answer their call and provide such blessings for the nation which he has made his own vineyard or planting.

The figure of being God's vineyard was often used of Israel, but is employed later by Paul in reference to the church (1 Cor 9:7). This is significant, since it shows that even now, God's people experience the fullness of his blessing (Eph 1:3); and just as Israel would never again be removed from the land which God gave to her, so those who are redeemed by the Lord will forever be acknowledged as his own people; and they shall own him as their God (Rev 21:3).

Chapter 3:1–5 God's Love for the Undeserving

3:1–2 The LORD said to me, "Go, show love to your wife again, even though she loves another man and continually commits adultery. Likewise, the LORD loves the Israelites although they turn to other gods and love to offer raisin cakes to idols." So I paid fifteen shekels of silver and about seven bushels of barley to purchase her.

After revealing in chapter two that his will and purpose for Israel was ultimately to restore her to himself, God directs Hosea on a course of action which would illustrate that purpose and demonstrate his love for Israel. In spite of all their backsliding, God still loved and would redeem his undeserving people. His instruction to Hosea signified this, for here God speaks of Israel, not as his "wife", but as "a woman"; she no longer deserved the title of "wife", and yet she was still loved as if she were a wife.

At this time Hosea's wife Gomer was living with one of her lovers. In order to demonstrate God's love for his unfaithful people, Hosea was instructed to go and bring Gomer back to his home. Hosea had loved Gomer when he married her; and it is clear that he still loved her in spite of her adulteries. It *cost* Hosea to get her back, for she had fallen so low that she had become the slave of the man she lived with. Hence Hosea had to pay the price of the slave, 30 shekels of silver, to redeem her; half of which he paid in cash and half in kind (Exod 21:32).

Hosea's action illustrates God's love not only for Israel, but also for the whole world. In spite of our sin, God continues to love all humanity (John 3:16). Although we had left God behind us in order to pursue our own way (Isa 53:6), God came to earth seeking for wayward humanity in the person of his Son, Jesus Christ. It was his purpose to redeem us and bring us home again to God. Christ demonstrated God's love for the undeserving and the unlovely (Rom 5:8). Just as Gomer we had become slaves to sin and Satan

(John 8:34); but Christ has redeemed us, his own death being the price which was paid to buy us back for God (Eph 1:7).

When a Jewish slave was redeemed, he did not then become the slave of his redeemer; instead he served for wages as a free man. So too Jesus Christ sets us free from slavery to sin, not that we might serve him under compulsion as his slave, but that we might serve him willingly, because of our love for him. We love him because he first loved us and redeemed us for God by his blood. Yet we must remember that since Christ has bought us we truly belong to him (1 Cor 6:20). Even so, belonging to the Lord and living for him is liberty, not slavery.

The law of Moses required that a divorced wife who had lived with another man could not return to her former husband (Deut 24:4); an edict which was confirmed many years later by Jeremiah (Jer 3:1). But as Tatford points out, "As for Israel, so for Gomer, grace was greater than law, and mercy went further than legal requirements."[9] So too with us, we receive grace and mercy rather than face the weight of the law against us the transgressors. Christ has satisfied the demands of the law so that he can give us what the law never could. We have received God's grace through righteousness, in order that we might be made righteous (Rom 5:21; John 1:14).

> *3:3 Then I told her, "You must live with me many days; you must not commit adultery or have sexual intercourse with another man, and I also will wait for you."*

To bring Gomer home was one thing, but to cure her of her desires for unfaithful and adulterous relationships was quite another. Guided by God, Hosea imposed a period of strict discipline to correct his erring wife. He placed her under a kind of house arrest. She was not to go out and mix with other people (Deut 21:13) and she was charged not to have sexual intercourse with any other man. Hosea in turn promised that he would not

---

[9] Tatford, 42

sleep with any other woman, nor would he resume conjugal relations with his wife until the period of discipline was over. The aim was to redirect Gomer's affections and desires back to her husband alone.

It must be stressed that this period of discipline was only for a time, until Hosea was satisfied that his wife would remain faithful to him. It is obviously not the normal state of any marriage, nor should it be. God's intention was that this should serve as a prophetic illustration of his dealings with Israel. Nevertheless, the immediate aim for Hosea's marriage was for the couple to be reconciled. The problems of Hosea's marriage are not unique. Almost all married couples experience problems of one sort or another during their married lives. Whilst the marriage guidance counsellor or the minister may be able to give advice, at the end of the day, only if the couple in question are both prepared to resolve their differences, and only if each is willing to give ground to the other, can progress be made to save a marriage in trouble. This passage of Hosea shows us that God's purpose is always directed toward reconciliation and for the mending of broken relationships.

Discipline and Restoration for the Erring Nation

> *3:4 For the Israelites must live many days without a king or prince, without sacrifice or sacred fertility pillar, without ephod or idols.*

Like Hosea with Gomer, God would impose a period of chastisement and discipline on the nation of Israel, after which Israel would return to him. They would experience a time of seclusion, away from their lovers, so that they might think about their attitudes and actions then return to the Lord. The "many days" spoken of were subsequent to the Assyrian invasion, when the land and people were largely destroyed and those who remained were taken into slavery in a foreign land. They would have no rulers, no kings or princes to lead them. They would have no religious form left to them, neither the sacrifices nor worship proscribed in the law, nor the idolatrous religion they had adopted in Canaan. None of this would be available to them, and they would have no one but God left to turn to. It was God's purpose that during this time the people might consider their sinful life choices, turn their hearts to seek God, and let their affections and desires be directed to him alone.

> *3:5 Afterward, the Israelites will turn and seek the LORD their God and their Davidic king. Then they will submit to the LORD in fear and receive his blessings in the future.*

At the end of this period of chastisement, God said that the nation of Israel would return and seek the Lord their God. It appears that this promise is yet to be completely fulfilled. For although the people of Israel did return to their land and rebuild their temple, they still failed to recognise or accept Christ when he came (John 1:11). Their temple was once again destroyed in 70 CE and their nation scattered again for an even longer period (from 70 to 1948 CE). Even up to the present time, although Israel has once again returned to the land, there has been no nationwide revival, no general acceptance of Christ as Saviour. However, a day is coming when the King mentioned here—a descendant of David—will come to take his throne, and the nation will accept him as their rightful king.

From the days of the Assyrian invasion until now, Israel has not had a king. Their king did come to them—he came in humility, bringing salvation and riding on a donkey (Zech 9:9)—but his people failed to recognise him. Together with their rulers they rejected and crucified him. Above his cross the title was written, "This is Jesus of Nazareth, King of the Jews" (John 19:19).

This Jesus, a descendant of David will one day return to claim his throne (2 Tim 2:8; Luke 1:32–33). This will happen in the latter days—at the end time—when the nation of Israel will receive Christ as Saviour, and so be born again. With renewed hearts they shall fear the Lord and his goodness to them; goodness like that which Joseph showed his estranged brothers.

Even though at first Joseph's brothers tried to kill him and sold him into slavery, yet later when he revealed himself to them as ruler of all Egypt, he forgave and provided for them (see Gen 45)—so will the coming King of Israel receive his repentant nation.

Both Jewish and Gentile Christians already know the Lord Jesus Christ and have experienced his salvation, and the new nature which we have received from him delights in the fear of the Lord. That is why we too will share in his glory and will reign with him upon the earth (Rev 5:10).

Chapter 4:1–19 God Goes to Court

The illustration drawn from Hosea's relationship with Gomer has now ended. It has served its purpose and is not mentioned again. From now on the prophet reverts to the more usual way of preaching to the people.

The Legal Case Against Israel

> *4:1–2 Hear the word of the LORD, you Israelites! For the LORD has a covenant lawsuit against the people of Israel. For there is neither faithfulness nor loyalty in the land, nor do they acknowledge God. There is only cursing, lying, murder, stealing, and adultery. They resort to violence and bloodshed.*

The Lord had a case to bring against his people, like a legal case being brought against someone in court. God is the plaintiff, the judge, and the lawgiver. God accuses his people of three sins of omission and five of commission, although these may be representative of their condition rather than a complete list of their failings.

Three Sins of Omission

Firstly, there was no faithfulness to God or man— no one could be trusted. Secondly, no loving kindness or mercy was shown to those in need. Thirdly, the worse omission which in fact gave rise to the other two—there was no knowledge of God in the land. Such ignorance was inexcusable, since God's covenant people had received the law through Moses. Yet the word of God had become so irrelevant to them that it was completely ignored. Many were not even aware of what the law required. The people knew little or nothing about their God, to the extent that false religion had taken over and become a national way of life.

Their Sins of Commission

Israel's sins of commission were just as bad: swearing, lying, killing, stealing, and adultery. There could be no doubt that God's law had been broken (Exod 20:13–16). By swearing, the prophet did not mean the use of bad language, but rather the taking of false oaths in the name of God. In modern courts, this is called "perjury" or lying to a court under oath. Lying was so commonplace in Israel during Hosea's lifetime that one would be shocked to hear a true word spoken. This was true in every area of life, in the home, in business, even in the place of worship.

No one could doubt the clarity of God's command, "do not kill" (Exod 20:13), but in the Israel of Hosea's day murder was common. If one man was angry with another then he would be ready to lash out, whether his anger was reasonable or not. The land was stained with bloodshed—a figure of its guilt. Only by the nation doing something to prevent these evils and reinstate justice and the rule of law could national guilt be expunged.

Amos had pointed out that the rich oppressed and took from the poor to become richer (e.g. Amos 2:6; 5:11). But the poor were guilty too; and how could the rulers, who were dishonest themselves, crack down on theft? So the increase in crime was left unchecked. The whole society became corrupt and selfish.

The religion in which the people were entangled was one which encouraged immorality. Sex with prostitutes in the temples was not so much an indulgence as an act of worship. Female prostitutes were on offer for the men and male prostitutes were available for the women. In such a prevailing atmosphere of immorality it is hardly surprising that adultery was commonplace. Sin had broken down the moral fabric of society until an "anything goes" culture prevailed. What a vivid picture of what are now accepted as modern cultural norms, especially in Western society!

> *4:3 Therefore the land will mourn, and all its inhabitants will perish. The wild animals, the birds of the sky, and even the fish in the sea will perish.*

Having found Israel guilty, the judge passes sentence. The law gave clear penalties for those who broke it. Among these were droughts, locusts, and loss of livestock. All these were to come upon Israel. The land and the animals that lived there would be affected as God meted out judgment on the people. Even the fish would die, as God withdrew this food supply from people's mouths.

> *4:4–5 Do not let anyone accuse or contend against anyone else: for my case is against you priests! You stumble day and night, and the false prophets stumble with you; You have destroyed your own people!*

As judgment fell, it was not time to lay blame on others. All the people were equally guilty. A similar teaching is found in the New Testament, for in Rom 3:23 Paul says that "all have sinned" and in Rom 2:1 he says, "*Therefore you are without excuse, whoever you are, when you judge someone else. For on whatever grounds you judge another, you condemn yourself, because you who judge practice the same things.*" Believers are warned not to take a judgmental attitude and apportion blame to others, whatever the circumstances (Matt 7:1–5); instead they are to ensure they are living right themselves.

The Failure of the Priesthood

> *4:6 You have destroyed my people by failing to acknowledge me! Because you refuse to acknowledge me, I will reject you as my priests. Because you reject the law of your God, I will reject your descendants.*

The priests were supposed to teach and instruct the people in the way of God and lead them by good example (Mal 2:7). Instead of this, the priests had led the people into idolatry, as had the so-called prophets who actually spoke in the name of Baal. Because of this neither priest nor prophet would be spared. Their entire families would be wiped out so that idolatry might be purged from Israel.

Had the priests instructed the people in the law and requirements of God, they would have returned to the Lord and repented of their sin. As it was, destruction had come upon them for lack of this knowledge. Those who were in possession of the truth and who could have instructed others chose rather to reject the truth for a lie. This wilful ignorance of what they knew to be God's Word made them guiltier. God would remove them from their priestly office. Although the priesthood was meant to be hereditary, they had forgotten the law given them by God and so God would forget their children—in other words, their children would not be priests after them; God would abolish the priesthood, and it would cease to function in Israel.

> *4:7–8 The more the priests increased in numbers, the more they rebelled against me. They have turned their glorious calling into a shameful disgrace! They feed on the sin offerings of my people; their appetites long for their iniquity!*

The priests made a lot of money from their false religion, and the more they had, the deeper they sank into sin as a means of making money. Their "glorious calling" was to lead many into righteousness, but instead they had led many into sin, which would be to their eternal shame (Dan 12:2–3). There is a great responsibility upon those who have spiritual leadership, and it is a devastating situation for such leaders to lead others into sin.

Because idolatrous religion brought them their income, they had a vested interest in the people continuing to sin. That is why God says, very literally, that they fed on the sin of his people, since they ate the sacrifices that were made to the golden calves. Tatford says, "There could scarcely be any greater impropriety than that of the priest, whose duty was to nurture the people in the faith, officially encouraging the transgressions of the sinner."[10] Neither the church nor its ministers should be guilty of condoning sin or of encouraging others to remain in their sins.

> *4:9–10 I will deal with the people and priests together: I will punish them both for their ways, and I will repay them for their deeds. They will eat, but not be satisfied; they will engage in prostitution, but not increase in numbers; because they have abandoned the LORD by pursuing other gods.*

Both the priests and the people would be punished together. Although the priests were guilty of leading the people into sin, that fact did not excuse the people of their own responsibility. Once again Hosea warns that God's retribution would involve famine—they shall eat but not be satisfied. The worship of Baal supposedly made the people and the land fertile, but now the land would be infertile and the people childless. The blessings, of food and of children, are bestowed by God. He would withdraw these blessings from an unthankful people who no longer paid any attention to his word.

Turning from God to Follow Demons

> *4:11–14 Old and new wine take away the understanding of my people. They consult their wooden idols, and their diviner's staff answers with an oracle. The wind of prostitution blows them astray; they commit spiritual adultery against their God. They sacrifice on the mountaintops, and burn offerings on the hills; they sacrifice under oak, poplar, and terebinth, because their shade is so pleasant. As a result, your daughters have become cult prostitutes, and your daughters-in-law commit adultery! I will not punish your daughters when they commit prostitution, nor your daughters-in-law when they commit adultery. For the men*

---

[10] Tatford, 60

consort with harlots, they sacrifice with temple prostitutes. It is true: "A people that lacks understanding will come to ruin!"

The people whom God had redeemed from Egypt, whom he had made his own, and to whom he had given his law, saw no visible form or figure of God when they received that law (Deut 4:1–2). Yet they had turned their backs on the living and true God. They no longer sought guidance from God, but from idols. They asked their blocks of wood for help and indeed their blocks of wood apparently answered them. Kiel tells us how this was done, "Two rods were held upright and then allowed to fall, while forms of incantation were being uttered; and the oracle was inferred from the way in which they fell."[11]

The Lord accuses his people of becoming stupid; their continual indulgence in sexual immorality and consuming alcohol had dulled their senses and robbed them of spiritual discernment (Eph 4:18). It also robbed them of self-respect and of respect for the marriage union. Sin takes its toll on the mind as well as the body.

Hosea makes plain that it was a spirit which had led them astray to worship idols rather than God. The New Testament confirms this truth: "You know that you were Gentiles, carried away to these dumb idols, even as you were led" (see 1 Cor 12:2; Eph 2:2 and 1 John 4:1). Demon spirits who do the bidding of their master Satan seek to blind men and women to the truth of God and lead them to an everlasting hell (2 Cor 4:4). These spirits also seek to disturb and distract God's own people and turn them away from following the truth (1 Tim 4:1 and 1 John 2:18).

The people of Israel had become pagans, worshipping the so-called gods of nature and natural forces. Many such deities were worshipped, known in plural as Baalim. The reference to shade illustrates how the people loved

---

[11] C. F. Kiel, The Twelve Minor Prophets, Vol. 1 (London: T&T Clark, 1878), 80. Cited by Tatford, 62

darkness rather than light, because their deeds were evil. The union of the men with shrine prostitutes set an example which was followed by their wives and daughters. That is why God says that he will hold the men, who were regarded as being at the head of each household, responsible for the situation. The tragic conclusion of this prophetic statement is that the people, being devoid of spiritual understanding, would be dashed to the ground. There was no hope for them. Their destruction was at hand.

A Warning Against Compromise

> *4:15 Although you, O Israel, commit adultery, do not let Judah become guilty! Do not journey to Gilgal! Do not go up to Beth Aven! Do not swear, "As surely as the LORD lives!"*

Here was a warning for Israel's neighbour Judah, not to follow Israel in the way of idolatry. The faithful people of Judah were warned to stay well away from the places where Israel kept her pagan shrines. This is a timely warning for us today. As Christians we must keep clear of anything that would lead us away from Jesus Christ. We must keep away from places where others indulge in pagan revelry, for we are not to associate with those who do such things (2 Cor 6:16–17). If this is the case, then we should carefully consider whether a drinking party or the sports team of the local pub is the right place for a Christian to be. Certainly the home of those who are involved in black arts or who claim to be in touch with demons is no place for a Christian, unless it is to bring deliverance in Jesus's name.

Hosea gave this warning because he knew that the influence on Judah would lead her astray from God. In fact, it later did. Christians should never compromise with sin and darkness, for eventually, such compromise will lead them away from God, back into sin, and ultimately to hell (2 Pet 2:20–21).

Israel Provides an Illustration of Apostasy

> *4:16–19 Israel has rebelled like a stubborn heifer! Soon the LORD will put them out to pasture like a lamb in a broad field! Ephraim has attached himself to idols; Do not go near him! They consume their alcohol, then engage in cult prostitution; they dearly love their shameful behavior. A whirlwind has wrapped them in its wings; they will be brought to shame because of their idolatrous worship.*

The prophet asks, "Should a cow that is prone to wandering be allowed to roam freely?" The answer is, of course not. Freedom and blessing were not suitable for a nation which, like an obstinate cow, was stubbornly rejecting the voice of God.

Ephraim is another name for Israel. She was irreparably joined to idols, and should be left alone to suffer the consequences of her sin. It is of note that Judah never fought to defend Israel. We can only do so much to help people. After that, we can only leave them to face the consequences of their folly.

When the people had finished drinking, they looked for immorality. The rulers were among those leading the way in this immoral behaviour. Because of this, Hosea, in remarkable picture language, speaks of the suddenness and violence with which Israel will be carried away to Assyria, like being caught up and carried away in a whirlwind which they would be helpless to resist.

Although they had known God, the nation of Israel had turned from him. This was a national apostasy. Only judgment could result. The apostate Christian is one who has known God, but who has now forsaken him and denies that he ever knew him. Nothing can await such a person but judgment (John 15:6).

Chapter 5:1–19 Ensnaring the Nation

Ensnaring the Nation

> *5:1–2 Hear this, you priests! Pay attention, you Israelites! Listen closely, O king! For judgment is about to overtake you! For you were like a trap to Mizpah, like a net spread out to catch Tabor. Those who revolt are knee-deep in slaughter, but I will discipline them all.*

God continues the legal case he began in chapter 4. The priests, the royal family, and the whole nation were all to be held guilty. Those in national and moral authority had led the way in corrupting the nation, and would now answer for this before God.

Mizpah, Tabor, and Shittim were centres of worship for the idolatrous cult of Baal. Once, God had been worshipped in these places; but the worship of the true God had been replaced by the worship of idols which were supposed to represent God. In a brief time, the significance of these idols had changed so that they had come to represent the gods of nature. The rulers had given their complete consent and support to this degradation of true religion and had given the cult of Baal their full patronage. It was the popular religion of the day; the "in thing" or the trendy thing to do. The example of the leaders had been followed by others, and in this way the leaders were responsible for the spiritual decline of the nation. Not only did they fail to uphold truth, morality, and the commandments of God, they had also set a trap to catch the unwary, that is, to entice them into Baal worship.

Hosea uses three illustrations to reveal how the people had been taken captive by this idolatrous religion. The snare or trap was used to catch birds one at a time. Thus individuals had been ensnared in Baal worship. Moreover, those who led the way in this backsliding had spread a net by which they had entangled the feet of the whole nation in idolatry. The third illustration is in verse two, which the American Standard Version translates as "and the revolters are gone deep in making slaughter." The idea is that of a deep pit which had been purposely dug to catch the hunted game. The leaders of the religious cult were guilty of forcibly converting people into their false religion. In all three illustrations, the idea conveyed is of the rulers being responsible for leading the people into the spiritual bondage of idolatry, just as a hunter is responsible for trapping an animal; and because of this God vows to punish them for their sin.

> *5:3-5 I know Ephraim all too well; the evil of Israel is not hidden from me. For you have engaged in prostitution, O Ephraim; Israel has defiled itself. Their wicked deeds do not allow them to return to their God; because a spirit of idolatry controls their heart, and they do not acknowledge the LORD. The arrogance of Israel testifies against it; Israel and Ephraim will be overthrown because of their iniquity. Even Judah will be brought down with them.*

God's judgment is always right and fair. He has no need to investigate or to provide the court with evidence to prove his charge; everything is known to him. God knows all that is done in secret as well as what is done in public. He knows everything that is in the hearts and minds of people. His knowledge is absolute, and it provides exhibit a, b, and c in heaven's court of law—evidence enough for a conviction.

God knew that the people of Israel were being unfaithful to him. They had rejected him, and did not want him as their God. That is why they had gone away from him to serve idols, a sin which corrupted the whole nation morally and spiritually.

Spiritual Bondage

Indeed, they had become bound by their deeds. Their sin had become to them like an iron chain from which they could not break free. Many people have, from painful experience, realised this same reality: that sin and iniquity will not release those who practice it (Eccl 8:8). Men and women are degraded and brought into captivity by sin, which is a hard task master; the only wages it pays is death (Rom 6:23). The bondage suffered is a spiritual one; people cannot be released from it by natural means. It was a *spirit* of idolatry which had fastened them in chains.

Behind the worship of Baal, its allurements and religious practices was the evil spirit of Satan, blinding and binding men, keeping them bound to sin and idolatry. In fact, it is only Jesus Christ that can set people free from the bondage of sin and Satan (John 8:34–36; Rom 6:17–18). His precious blood makes us free. "All praise to him who always loves us and who set us free from our sins by pouring out his lifeblood for us." (Rev 1:5 Living Bible)

As Christians we must beware of anything that might bring us into spiritual bondage. Jesus Christ has set us free from sin, so let us not allow ourselves to become entangled in it again (2 Pet 2:20; Gal 5:1). If we are bound by evil habits, or even by inappropriate relationships with ungodly people, then we must remember that the matter is a spiritual one. Our deliverance will involve both confession and repentance—for only Christ can set us free.

One of the effects of being in bondage to sin is ignorance. The Lord alleges that "they do not acknowledge [or know] the LORD" (see Eph 4:18). Their hearts have become hardened by sin, and consequently they have become blind to spiritual reality.

It was because of the pride of the nation, their stubbornness and hardness of heart, that they refused to repent at the command of God's prophets. This rejection of God's word and his messengers would in and of itself have resulted in their condemnation. This warning is relevant today for all those who will not listen to someone who is greater than any prophet—God's Son Jesus Christ (John 3:18; Heb 12:25).

Their rejection of God and his mercy would be their ruin. It could be said that no one goes to hell because of their sin, but because they refuse to receive the remedy for their sin which God makes available through faith in Jesus Christ.

Too Late!

> *5:6–7 Although they bring their flocks and herds to seek the favor of the LORD, They will not find him—he has withdrawn himself from them! They have committed treason against the LORD, because they bore illegitimate children. Soon the new moon festival will devour them and their fields.*

We have mentioned that originally the centres of idolatry were meant to be centres of worship to God. Now God declares that when the people come to seek him there and offer sacrifice, he will not hear them. They have hardened their hearts and rejected his word. It is too late.

No one can come to God on their own terms. We can only come to God on his terms and in his time. God is not obligated to show mercy to any one of us. Salvation is the sovereign act of a merciful God; all may receive it, yet none deserve it. Israel had been given the opportunity to repent, but this opportunity had been rejected. Now it was too late. Unbelievers should be aware of the scripture which warns that one day the day of grace will end, all opportunity to be saved will have gone and there will be no hope for the unrepentant (2 Cor 6:2).

The Lord had removed his presence, blessing, and protection from Israel. She had been unfaithful to him (the word translated "treason" or "treachery" actually refers to spiritual adultery, which is unfaithfulness to God), as was evidenced by the fact that they had brought up pagan children. The people had departed so far from the Lord that their children, the children of God's special covenant people, knew nothing of Jehovah and were neither more nor less than pagan.

Such a terrible indictment could also be made of the UK today. When we see that children have little or no knowledge of the scripture, of God, or the moral and spiritual absolutes of his kingdom, then we must realize that this is damning evidence against a generation who have departed from the living God.

The last part of verse 7 is difficult. The new moon was associated with religious festivals. The verse could mean that judgment would overtake them before the next new moon, i.e. within a month, but this is unlikely. It is more probable that the prophet intends to show how pagan religion itself, symbolised by its observance of the phases of the moon, would bring about the destruction of Israel.

No different sentence can be pronounced on our own nation. It is as guilty as Israel of idolatry and unfaithfulness to God. Judgment is inevitable for every unrepentant sinner. The only thing that causes God to withhold his punishment is his love and patience; giving his church opportunity to preach the way of salvation through Jesus Christ in the hope that some may come to repentance and escape the wrath to come.

Sound The Alarm!

> *5:8 Blow the ram's horn in Gibeah! Sound the trumpet in Ramah! Sound the alarm in Beth Aven! Tremble in fear, O Benjamin!*

The sounding of the trumpet at these key cities would send warning to the whole nation of impending military invasion. This language is employed to warn the people that a terrible invasion was indeed coming; and it was the hand of God that brought it.

> *5:9–11 Ephraim will be ruined in the day of judgment! What I am declaring to the tribes of Israel will certainly take place! The princes of Judah are like those who move boundary markers. I will pour out my rage on them like a torrential flood! Ephraim will be oppressed, crushed under judgment, because he was determined to pursue worthless idols.*

Such would be the power of God's rebuke that the nation would be ravaged by war. No attempt to secure support from foreign allies would avail; God's mind would not be changed. When God says something will happen then it will surely come to pass. God has all knowledge, so when he speaks, he does not need to change his plans. Nothing ever "occurs" to God. He has all power. No one can stop God from accomplishing his purpose. Because he is eternal whilst we are in time, every point of the world's history has already happened from his point of view, so that God may report the future as accurately as we might report the recent past.

Instead of being warned by the punishment of Israel, the leaders of Judah remained unconcerned about following her into sin; being concerned only with taking advantage of Israel's plight and securing parts of the land for themselves. Therefore, God says he would pour out his judgment on them like a torrent of water.

The disaster which befell Israel came because of her stubbornly refusing to listen to God and persisting wilfully to worship idols despite many warnings. The corresponding indictment against Judah was that the example made of Israel was not sufficient to deter Judah from following the same downward path. The idolatry of Judah ultimately resulted in her destruction by the Babylonians in 597 BCE.

Destruction of a Nation: but a Remnant Will Return

> *5:12–15 I will be like a moth to Ephraim, like wood rot to the house of Judah. When Ephraim saw his sickness and Judah saw his wound, then Ephraim turned to Assyria, and begged its great king for help. But he will not be able to heal you! He cannot cure your wound! I will be like a lion to Ephraim, like a young lion to the house of Judah. I myself will tear them to pieces, then I will carry them off, and no one will be able to rescue them! Then I will return again to my lair until they have suffered their punishment. Then they will seek me; in their distress they will earnestly seek me.*

As a moth consumes a garment, or wet or dry rot destroys timber until it is completely eaten away, so the prophet indicates that God would be responsible for the destruction of the nation. When the time came for Israel and Judah to realise that judgment was imminent, even then they would not turn from the sin which caused their destruction. Instead of turning to God for mercy they both made pacts and agreements with the warlike kings of Assyria, which they hoped would save them from the threatened assault. They relied on the arm of flesh and did not trust in God. But the arm of flesh failed them.

We too should beware of relying on our own strength, ability, or cleverness rather than God. The King of Assyria could not remove the root cause of the nation's distress. Only turning to God in sincere repentance could have done that. So now they would be made to see the folly of their ways. In spite of all their human strength, God would accost them like a roaring hungry lion to bring wounding and suffering to the nation, causing those who remained to be taken as captives to a foreign land. Then, says God, he would return to his own place (his lair). This might be taken as a reference to the temple, except that the temple itself was later destroyed. It is more likely to be a figure of speech meaning that God would again patiently wait for the people to confess their sin and repent, seeking his face earnestly.

Indeed, this is exactly what the prophet predicts they would do earnestly and sincerely amid the affliction which resulted from the dispersion of Israel and the exile of Judah which followed the destruction of Samaria and Jerusalem respectively. Although only a remnant would survive, God's action in correcting the people would be seen to have its desired effect. The hearts of the exiles would repent and turn to God. For an example of this, consider the prayer of the exiled Nehemiah (Neh 1:5–9) or that of Daniel (Dan 9:3–19).

Chapter 6:1–11 A Song of Repentance

A Song of Repentance

> *6:1–3 "Come on! Let's return to the LORD! He himself has torn us to pieces, but he will heal us! He has injured us, but he will bandage our wounds! He will restore us in a very short time; he will heal us in a little while, so that we may live in his presence. So let us acknowledge him! Let us seek to acknowledge the LORD! He will come to our rescue as certainly as the appearance of the dawn, as certainly as the winter rain comes, as certainly as the spring rain that waters the land."*

These few verses are in fact the words of a penitential Psalm, which most probably was sung by the prophet as an exhortation to God's people. The song offers genuine hope to those who were prepared to humble themselves and turn from their sin. From the words of this song, we understand that when the people sinned, it was God who brought affliction on them as a form of chastisement. The trouble Israel faced came not as a result of bad luck, or the work of the devil, but from the hand God; the national chastisement was God's way of bringing them back to himself.

This is an important lesson for all Christians to learn. A loving father will correct his children when they do wrong; even so, when God's children go astray, any trouble which he may bring on them is intended to lead them back into the right way. It is important that we neither ignore nor rebel against God's chastisement (Heb 12:5–6).

When the chastisement had achieved its desired effect, the people were prepared to take steps to return to God. Then (as in the parable of the prodigal son in Luke 15), they would be welcomed by the arms of their ever-loving Father. In the parable of Jesus, the prodigal's fellowship with his father was restored as soon as he returned home. His acceptance was immediate. Restoration to fellowship with God would be swift for the repentant, just as it is for any penitent sinner who comes to Jesus and receives him as Saviour. Immediately, when someone receives Christ as Saviour, their sins are forgiven and they enter into a new and living relationship with God.

The father of the prodigal son said "My son was dead and is alive again" (Luke 15:24). Hosea says the same thing, that when God's people return to him he will "raise them up" that they might live in his sight. This teaching is made even clearer by the New Testament. Those outside of Christ are dead in their trespasses and sins; spiritually dead (Eph 2:1). They need to be raised to life by receiving the spiritual life that God's son Jesus Christ provides. Whenever a person receives Christ as their Saviour they are raised from spiritual death to spiritual life (Eph 2:5). They are born again and have the life of God living within them. Only Jesus can give life in place of death (John 5:21). Having received this new life, we are raised to a new position, being seated in heavenly places in Christ Jesus (Eph 2:6).

When the prodigal son returned home, he offered to become his father's slave, saying "I am no longer worthy to be called your son." Instead of taking up his son's offer to become a servant, the father immediately took him back as his son again. All those who believe and receive Jesus Christ as saviour become sons of God (Gal 3:26; John 1:12). We do not have to prove ourselves, trying to become holy before God will accept us, for when we come trusting in Jesus, we are (by grace) "accepted in the beloved" (Eph 1:6). The basis of our acceptance with God is that Christ died for our sins and was raised from the dead. Given that the words translated "in a very short time ... in a little while" in the NET above are literally "after two days ... on the third day" (an expression was commonly used to imply that something would happen soon), Matthew Henry believes that verse 2 may be a reference to the resurrection of Christ after three days. Whether this is so or not, it is certainly because of Jesus's death and resurrection that we can die to sin and live for God (Rom 6:4).

Returning to the context of the passage, Hosea's song gives genuine hope to God's people: just as there is chastisement when we sin, so there is forgiveness and healing when we return to God. But Hosea's song also made clear that repentance must result in renewed consecration to God. True repentance will always result in a changed heart and life. It would be wrong to preach "come to Jesus today, believe in him and you'll be saved, then go back to your old way of life and do exactly what you want to do as you did before." This in no way reflects the teaching of the Lord Jesus Christ who advocated a life of discipleship through following the principles set out in the New Testament.

When we receive Jesus Christ as our Lord and Saviour we are surrendering our hearts, lives, and will entirely to him; no longer to live for ourselves but for him who died for us and rose again (Rom 14:9; 2 Cor 5:15). The result of our salvation is a complete change of life, as we are made "new creations" in Christ (2 Cor 5:7). As we desire to know God's will for our lives we will begin to live in a way that pleases him. Hosea describes this as a "following on to know the Lord" (AV). Jesus never called his disciples just to believe in him, then go home and forget him. He said "follow me."

Like the children of Israel in Hosea's day, we must learn that genuine repentance must lead to following Christ day by day. The promises given those who do so are tremendous. Hosea sings that "his going forth is sure as the morning: and he shall come unto us as the rain, as the latter rain that water the earth" (RV). Because of the Lord's constant love and mercy, "his mercies are new every morning" (Lam 3:22–23). God would refresh, renew, and revive his repentant people spiritually; just as the winter and spring rains soften the ground and make it fruitful. What Hosea is saying is that God's purpose in blessing his people is to make them fruitful (Acts 3:19). For ultimately, only fruitfulness is pleasing to God; in this context "fruitfulness" has to do with holiness of living and Christ-likeness of character and is not explicitly a reference to material blessing or even to the results of evangelism (Rom 6:22).

Superficial or True Devotion?

> *6:4-6 What am I going to do with you, O Ephraim? What am I going to do with you, O Judah? For your faithfulness is as fleeting as the morning mist; it disappears as quickly as dawn's dew! Therefore, I will certainly cut you into pieces at the hands of the prophets; I will certainly kill you in fulfillment of my oracles of judgment; for my judgment will come forth like the light of the dawn. For I delight in faithfulness, not simply in sacrifice; I delight in acknowledging God, not simply in whole burnt offerings*

God's complaint is that in spite of all his goodness to Israel, her devotion was nothing more than an early morning mist, which the morning sun soon dried up as if it had never been there. It came and went as quickly as it appeared.

As Christians we must beware of this same fault. We might be full of God when taking part in public meetings, or when we are excited about how God is using us; but what are we like when other Christians are not around to see us? What are we like when God is not noticeably using us? Are we full of God and faithful to him in those times too? A Christian must behave as a Christian whether in the company of believers or unbelievers; during good times and hard times. Unfortunately, Jesus said that some would only choose to be identified as his followers when it suited them (Matt 13:20-21).

Because of Israel's unfaithfulness, God had sent his prophets to speak to them, to make them change their ways, rather like a stone mason uses a hammer and chisel to fashion stones in a way that is useful to him. But since the stones would not take shape they had to be rejected.

The word of God became to them a message of death leading to death, for they heard God's word, but did not obey it. Those who were rejected by God were those who had first rejected God. The last part of verse 5 tells us the tragic result of their rejection: "Suddenly, without warning, my judgment will strike you as surely as day follows night" (LIVING BIBLE).

In chapter 5, we discussed the people's superficial drawing near to God. This had involved sacrifice, but sacrifice was not what God wanted from them. Instead he desired piety, which is heartfelt love and devotion for God born out of contrition for sin and a gratitude to God for his forgiveness. This was absent in the Israel of Hosea's day. It was absent from the scribes and Pharisees in Jesus's day. They offered sacrifices and did many other "religious" things—yet these meaningless rituals did not please God, and only brought them a stinging rebuke from Christ.

Christ taught that heartfelt love and devotion for God, resulting in a love for people was what mattered (Matt 9:13). Knowledge of God's person and will, resulting in heartfelt obedience to him, were far more important than burnt sacrifice. A scribe in Jesus's day understood this (Mark 12:33); King Saul did not (1 Sam 15:22).

Wickedness in the Land

> *6:7 At Adam they broke the covenant; Oh how they were unfaithful to me!*

God laments that although the people were told what to do, they did not do it. Instead, they were unfaithful to him and broke his laws continually; just as the first man Adam had done, in breaking God's command (Gen 3:17) and as we have all done ever since (Rom 3:23).

> *6:8–9 Gilead is a city full of evildoers; its streets are stained with bloody footprints! The company of priests is like a gang of robbers, lying in ambush to pounce on a victim. They commit murder on the road to Shechem; they have done heinous crimes!*

Two wicked cities come in for special mention. Gilead was a place where lawless bandits and murderers had made their home; it was not safe to travel there. Nor was it safe to go to Shechem, where gangs of murderous bandits lay in wait for innocent passers-by. Among these men were priests of the Baalim cult. Tatford says that "this depraved troop murdered, raped, and outraged at will. The word translated [heinous crimes], referred particularly to ... [sexual assault and rape]."[12]

> *6:10 I have seen a disgusting thing in the temple of Israel: there Ephraim practices temple prostitution and Judah defiles itself. I have appointed a time to reap judgment for you also, O Judah!*

Yet if Gilead and Shechem were representative of the evil in the land, God had seen something even more deplorable. Literally "something that would make your hair stand on end." Not only in isolated towns, but throughout the whole nation, Israel had turned from the God who had brought her out of Egypt and given her the land in which she lived. Immorality had become commonplace; but in God's eyes the most abhorrent thing was Israel's wilful rejection of the Living God.

Today, many people believe that they are living respectable lives. Many have never been in trouble with the law, or done anyone any harm. Nevertheless, the tragedy is that such people will go to hell if they do not receive Christ as Lord and Saviour (John 3:18), for the rejection of God and of Christ is the worst of all crimes. So, says Hosea, a day of harvest, a reaping for the nation had been determined—a time when the nation would reap the fruit of its evil doing. It would be a day of judgment when Israel would be taken into captivity. Not only Israel but Judah too, who had not kept herself free of the pollution's of her neighbour, would suffer punishment. When they saw what happened to Israel because of her sin, they did not repent, but became worse than Israel. For this reason, God would send Judah into exile to Babylon.

---

[12] Tatford, 86

Chapter 7:1–16 Spiritual Healing

God's Way for Spiritual Healing

> *7:1 Whenever I want to heal Israel, the sin of Ephraim is revealed, and the evil deeds of Samaria are exposed. For they do what is wrong; thieves break into houses, and gangs rob people out in the streets.*

In order to heal Israel, God first of all had to make her realise the true nature of her spiritual condition. He did this by sending the prophets who highlighted the ways in which the people were sinning against God. Unfortunately, although the people were very religious, their religion proved to be a sham; it was fake, focussing on Baal and not the heart-felt worship of Yahweh. The people of Israel were religious but not righteous; pious but not truly God-honouring. Instead of responding to the word of God given by the prophets with repentance and obedience they continued to rebel. Indeed, such was the evil environment which they had created that burglary and highway robbery flourished in the land.

> *7:2 They do not realize that I remember all of their wicked deeds. Their evil deeds have now surrounded them; their sinful deeds are always before me.*

The reason that Israel paid no heed to the word of God and the warnings of the prophets was that they did not believe them. Like many people today, either they did not accept the fact that at some future time they would give an account of themselves to God, or they simply did not care about it. Nevertheless, it remains true that each person must one day give an account of themselves to God (Rom 14:11; Matt 12:36).

God saw that the people were "surrounded" by their sins; held captive in bondage and unable to free themselves from sin. Such is the situation for all those outside of Jesus Christ; they are slaves of sin (John 8:34; Rom

6:16). Outside of Christ we are all in this bondage (Eph 2:1–3), and only Christ can set us free (John 8:36; Rom 6:17–18). The importance of being delivered from our sins through faith in Christ cannot be stressed to highly, for God has a record of every sin which every person has ever committed and one day he will judge all people for their sins (Rev 20:12). How many people today, like the people of Israel in Hosea's time, fail to heed the warnings of the God's word concerning future judgment? Why do they refuse to believe in the inescapable truth? Because to accept it would mean that they would have to repent, change their ways and seek God for mercy—things which they are not prepared to do. So, because of their impenitent heart, they "store up wrath for themselves against the day of wrath and revelation of the righteous judgment of God" (Rom 2:5).

God's way for spiritual healing has not changed and still provides the answer for the world's greatest need today. However, men and women must first be made aware of and realise their sinful condition before the remedy for sin and granting of pardon through faith in his Son the Lord Jesus Christ can be effective.

The Rule of Anarchy

> *7:3 The royal advisers delight the king with their evil schemes, the princes make him glad with their lies.*

One of the reasons why crime, especially burglary, flourished was that it was unchecked by Israel's rulers. Since all the leaders cared about was their own pleasures, they failed to govern the country as they ought. They were glad to see the people's wickedness since it provided a cloak for their own.

When a nation has turned its back on God and has accepted lower moral standards, ungodly leaders are pleased, for they will then be allowed to indulge their own pleasures without opposition from the people.

7:4 They are all like bakers, they are like a smoldering oven; they are like a baker who does not stoke the fire until the kneaded dough is ready for baking.

The sin of sexual immorality was especially rife in the land. Hosea describes the whole nation as being as hot as a pre-heated oven, so much did they burn in lust. The same vice is common today. Men and women consider faithfulness to one's marriage partner to be unfashionable, and it has become a socially accepted norm for people to have several partners before marriage. What is more they think nothing of having one or more sexual relationships during marriage with someone other than their own spouse. In the society in which we live wrong is hailed as right and right is rejected as wrong. The Christian must pay attention to the word of God about sexual relationships rather than to the accepted cultural norm as portrayed in the media; obedience to the word of God leads to blessing. Paul advises men and women that it is better to marry than to burn with lust (1 Cor 7:9); for within marriage, the sexual relationship between husband and wife is pure and holy (Heb 13:4). There are serious implications for the man or woman, says Jesus, who splits up a marriage by adultery (Matt 19:6).

Unfaithfulness to one's marriage partner is a sin against God. Paul offers some immensely candid and practical advice (it is advice, rather than the command of God) to Christian married couples. He suggests that they should ensure that they have sexual intercourse as frequently as either partner wishes. This is in order to reduce the possible temptation placed on either partner to seek this pleasure elsewhere (1 Cor 7:5).

7:5 At the celebration of their king, his princes become inflamed with wine; they conspire with evildoers.

Over indulgence with alcohol was another outstanding factor of the nation's apostasy. Even the king and the princes, on national feast days, rather than honouring God with their sacrifices, praise and thanksgiving, got drunk, even drinking until they were sick (Prov 23:29–30). Whilst such behaviour is common in our Western culture today, Christians are warned against drunkenness, which leads to acts of sin (Eph 5:18).

> *7:6–7 They approach him, all the while plotting against him. Their hearts are like an oven; their anger smolders all night long, but in the morning it bursts into a flaming fire. All of them are blazing like an oven; they devour their rulers. All of their kings fall—and none of them call on me!*

However, there was method behind the actions of the princes. They were not trying to get the king or his advisors drunk for fun. Evil plots burned in their hearts to kill him and seize his power. History records that during this period, following the death of Jeroboam II, one after another the kings of Israel were murdered. The intrigue which led to these deaths continued until the anarchy which heralded the end of the nation set in prior to the invasion of Assyria. Yet despite this situation, there was not a single person in government office who called on God for mercy on behalf of the nation.

Unfaithfulness to God was the Cause of Israel's Weakness

> *7:8 Ephraim has mixed itself like flour among the nations; Ephraim is like a ruined cake of bread that is scorched on one side.*

It was because Israel had mingled herself with the nations and adopted their sinful and idolatrous practices that she had become so unpalatable to God; rather like a cake burned on one side and uncooked on the other.

A similar illustration is used by the Lord Jesus Christ when speaking to the lukewarm, worldly church of Laodicea (Rev 3:15–16). The Christians in Laodicea had allowed material things to take their eyes from the Lord. Rather than being on fire for God, they craved a comfortable life of comparative wealth and ease.

Jesus said to them, "Because you are lukewarm I will spit you out of my mouth." In just the same way Christians today can become unpalatable to the Lord and useless to him because of their worldliness.

> *7:9–10 Foreigners are consuming what his strenuous labor produced, but he does not recognize it! His head is filled with gray hair, but he does not realize it! The arrogance of Israel testifies against him, yet they refuse to return to the LORD their God! In spite of all this they refuse to seek him!*

It was Israel's mixing with the nations that led to her weakness. Rather than rely on God in times of national trouble, they had paid tribute and sought to make peace treaties with foreign kings. All of this backfired on them, for God alone was to be their strength and their relationship with him was to be their security. Politically and morally, the signs of decay were evident in the nation; so much so that anyone could have realised that the end was near. But Israel did not realise. The grey hairs of a man's head show him that old age and ultimately death are on the way. But because of their pride, Israel failed to recognise the warning signs which God had given them so they and did not turn to God in repentance.

> *7:11–12 Ephraim has been like a dove, easily deceived and lacking discernment. They called to Egypt for help; they turned to Assyria for protection. I will throw my bird net over them while they are flying, I will bring them down like birds in the sky; I will discipline them when I hear them flocking together.*

God illustrates the folly of the nation, who will seek help from their neighbouring superpowers, but will not ask for help from almighty God. Because of this, God would make sure that the help of the nations was of no use to Israel at all, and he would punish them just as the prophets had warned. God would teach Israel that their help came only from God.

> *7:13 Woe to them! For they have fled from me! Destruction to them! For they have rebelled against me! I want to deliver them, but they have lied to me.*

The woe pronounced is because Israel had fled from God, abandoning him as a bird flies the nest. Their sin against God had brought about their own destruction as a nation. They had been unfaithful to the one who had redeemed them and brought them out of Egypt; who gave them the land in which they lived. Instead of worshipping him, they had attributed all these blessings to their idols, so now God would take back the land and send them once again into slavery.

> *7:14 They do not pray to me, but howl in distress on their beds; They slash themselves for grain and new wine, but turn away from me.*

In the trouble which the nation faced, they had not called upon God, although they had cried aloud and spent sleepless nights in anxiety about what was happening to them, and about where their food was going to come from. Instead, they sought the favour and blessing of their idols in order to obtain grain and oil. In doing this they wilfully rebelled against the chastening hand of God, who had brought this trouble upon them to bring them back to him. This was not ignorance but stubbornness.

The New Testament similarly warns believers not to rebel against the chastening hand of God (Heb 12:5–6). The history of the nation of Israel illustrates that there is a difference between true repentance and sorrow for sin, and mere regret at the loss or pain which sin has caused (cf. Rev 16:10–11).

> *7:15 Although I trained and strengthened them, they plot evil against me!*

Whether by chastising or by strengthening them, Israel remained estranged from their God. Despite all God's efforts to bring the nation back to him, nothing had worked. This is the way in which they had become useless, good for nothing, and nothing more could be done with them other than the outpouring of judgment which Hosea had already warned them about.

> *7:16 They turn to Baal; they are like an unreliable bow. Their leaders will fall by the sword because their prayers to Baal have made me angry. So people will disdain them in the land of Egypt.*

In their distress, the people did not turn to God for help, but to their idols and their foreign allies. Yet these could not and did not help them, any more than a bow which misfires is of any help to its archer. God would ensure that the rulers of Israel would pay for their blasphemy and arrogant speeches against him and he would bring such disaster on them that would cause their neighbours the Egyptians to ridicule them as a nation.

Chapter 8:1–14 God's Word Despised

8:1 Sound the alarm! An eagle looms over the temple of the LORD! For they have broken their covenant with me, and have rebelled against my law.

Hosea was told to set the trumpet to his mouth—a trumpet blast was a warning signal, the sign of an impending invasion. It was by these words that God warned Israel of the impending invasion of the Assyrians, who would come like a bird of prey to tear the guilty nation because of its sin. Some translators have chosen to render the bird of prey referred to as a vulture. Vultures only eat dead flesh and by continually sinning, violating the covenant, and breaking the laws of God Israel could aptly be referred to as "dead meat", for they had shown themselves to be "dead in trespasses and sins" (Eph 2:1).

8:2-3 Israel cries out to me, "My God, we acknowledge you!" But Israel has rejected what is morally good; so an enemy will pursue him.

Israel cried out to God, but in pretence. Claiming to know him with religious language, they actually denied him by their impious actions. The life they lived proved that they did not have an experimental knowledge of Jehovah. God desires reality and sincerity in the lives of his people (see Luke 13:25-27).

They did not accept his teaching or walk in his ways. They loathed what was right, and considered the holy precepts of God to be wrong. Indeed, in v. 11-13 God says that although he had given them his law and the many rules for life and conduct which it contained, they had regarded God's word as something strange, old fashioned, and irrelevant.

We can see the same thing in our present day. People are not only unconcerned about the word of God; they openly scorn it. Occasionally we may see letters in newspapers, declaring the need for the biblical values to be upheld; but invariably these letters are scorned and ridiculed by other writers, editors or politicians. When campaigners for morality oppose the media's craving for ever more sex, violence, and excessive bad language, they are almost universally branded bigoted; whilst those of senior years are thought of as "fuddy-duddies", prudes who need rescuing from their morals.

The enemies of righteousness refuse to accept that those who speak out for truth are seeking the welfare of young people, being fully aware of the consequences of promiscuity in this life and the next.

Like many modern Western countries, the UK is in an alarmingly similar condition to Israel in Hosea's time. Then, the law of God was considered an alien thing as it is today. Israel had rejected what was morally good, and it was because of this that Hosea declared God's judgment; the nation was about to be overthrown by disaster and forced to flee from its enemies.

> *8:4 They enthroned kings without my consent! They appointed princes without my approval! They made idols out of their silver and gold, but they will be destroyed!*

At the highest level of national and political life, the people did not consult God or his word. Leaders and kings were appointed as the people saw fit without inquiring of God. In this way they had severed the cord between themselves and heaven. God scathingly says "I didn't even know about it", "I was last to know." Of course, this is a figure of speech, for God knows everything, but it illustrates that the people were not in a correct and intimate relationship with God. They had put God behind them and lived their lives without him.

Instead of worshipping and obeying the true God, they had made idols of silver and gold to help them forget the reality of the one whose laws they hated and whom they had rejected. This made their sin complete and led to them being cut off as a nation; for since they had severed links with God, God would sever links with them.

8:5-6 O Samaria, he has rejected your calf idol! My anger burns against them! They will not survive much longer without being punished, even though they are Israelites! That idol was made by a workman — it is not God! The calf idol of Samaria will be broken to bits.

The god which Israel had chosen for itself was a golden calf. To God this was repulsive. It denigrated his deity, reducing the Eternal to the level of a creature which he had made. This breach of the first and second commandment caused God's anger to burn against the people, as it did at Sinai (Exod 32:8-10). For it was at Sinai that Israel had first made a calf for itself to worship and they had continued their idolatry ever since. How long would it be, asks God, before they put idolatry away from them and become pure in his sight? How long could they be so blind? The craftsman who made the idol was only a man, and if the idol was manmade, how could it possibly be a god? It certainly was not the true God, and the indestructible God would see to it that this idol was broken to pieces.

Reaping the Consequences

8:7 They sow the wind, and so they will reap the whirlwind! The stalk does not have any standing grain; it will not produce any flour. Even if it were to yield grain, foreigners would swallow it all up.

Here is the rule of cause and effect. Hosea says that the nation had sown the wind and would reap the whirlwind. Since in their spiritual lives, Israel had chosen to worship a useless idol, they themselves had become barren and useless. They would be punished by overwhelming destruction. Both Jesus and John the Baptist used illustrations which have a strikingly similar meaning when they both said, "Every tree that does not bear good fruit is cut down and thrown into the fire" (Matt 3:10; 7:19). Israel had not produced the fruit of lives which were obedient and pleasing to God, but had lived fruitless lives far from God. The fruitless tree was to be uprooted and destroyed.

Because of their sin, their crops would fail (a total disaster for an agrarian community such as Israel) and if any food were to be found for them, this would be destroyed or consumed by the invading army from Assyria.

> *8:8–10 Israel will be swallowed up among the nations; they will be like a worthless piece of pottery. They have gone up to Assyria, like a wild donkey that wanders off. Ephraim has hired prostitutes as lovers. Even though they have hired lovers among the nations, I will soon gather them together for judgment. Then they will begin to waste away under the oppression of a mighty king.*

Just as their food was swallowed up so the nation itself was to be swallowed up. They would be over-run, captured, and sent into exile. In this way they would be scattered among the nations. They had been chosen to be the special people of God; but the vessel that was meant to bring honour was now reduced to being a vessel of dishonour. Israel was like a common pottery mug which its owner might readily discard.

Israel had paid tribute to Assyria in return for their military help; they had also made a treaty which supposedly guaranteed that Assyria would not invade Israel. Because of this, God accuses them of being as stubborn as a mule, taking their own wilful way and not his. God had told Israel that the only way to avoid Assyrian invasion was to repent and return to him; but instead of this, they tried to buy peace for themselves.

Their plan did not work; they had spent their money in vain, for God would see to it that his word was fulfilled. It was he who lay behind the judgment which would soon overtake them. Therefore, it was not time for diplomatic negotiations or discussions with the enemy, but for direct discussions with the God who alone could save them.

When judgment came upon them, God would for a time remove the Davidic dynasty. Yet this was only to be for a little while in God's sight. A future day was promised by Ezekiel when the nation of Israel will be reunited with Judah (Ezek 37:16–22). At that time, rather than appoint their own kings, they would accept the king whom God had chosen from eternity and anointed—the Lord Jesus Christ. Today Israel and Judah are united in the land, yet the majority of the nation remains in unbelief with regard to Jesus. Of course, many Jews throughout history have come to faith in Christ, but Israel as a whole never has. Yet one day, when Jesus returns to earth to reign, I submit that the whole nation of Israel (that is, those who are alive at that time) will receive and welcome him.

A Backslidden People

> *8:11–13 Although Ephraim has built many altars for sin offerings, these have become altars for sinning! I spelled out my law for him in great detail, but they regard it as something totally unknown to them! They offer up sacrificial gifts to me, and eat the meat, but the LORD does not accept their sacrifices. Soon he will remember their wrongdoing, he will punish their sins, and they will return to Egypt.*

The people had built many altars on which to offer sacrifices for sin to appease God. Later, when the worship of God was abandoned, these altars had become centres of idolatry. The sacrifices supposedly offered for sin were eaten by the worshippers, most probably in drunken revelry as they engaged in the immoral sexual rites of the fertility cult associated with Baal. Thus the play on words; the altars for sin had become altars for sinning. They enjoyed their sin, even as they supposedly offered sacrifices to atone for it. Thus God refused to accept the people or their so called sacrifices, which were not made with a broken or contrite heart (Ps 51:16–17).

The time had come for God to remember and punish their sins by taking them back into captivity and slavery. The text may mean that they were to return to the condition of slavery in which they had been in Egypt rather than to that nation literally. However, during the dispersion it seems that some did settle in Egypt (Zech 10:10).

Believers today must heed the unchanging truth which lies behind this warning. God has brought us from spiritual darkness into light and from slavery to sin to freedom in Christ. However, if we turn away from God, despise his word, and become idolaters, then our last condition is worse than the first. We will have irrevocably returned to bondage (2 Pet 2:20–21).

> *8:14 Israel has forgotten his Maker and built royal palaces, and Judah has built many fortified cities. But I will send fire on their cities; it will consume their royal citadels.*

Somehow the nation had come to believe that it could live without God. Many people think the same today. Israel thought that by building strong cities and defences that they could deliver themselves from any attack. But their confidence was unfounded. The very defences on which they relied would be swept away in God's judgment. Indeed, it would have been far better for the nation to have had no defences at all and yet to have God on their side than to turn their backs on their almighty defender.

The question for those who live independently of God is "what defence will save you from the wrath of God?" The only refuge for sinners is the Lord Jesus Christ. Only in him are we safe eternally, and I would urge the reader to take refuge in him.

Chapter 9:1–17 Israel's Punishment

Because of her sin, Israel is to suffer: the loss of material blessings, the loss of spiritual blessings, and the loss of children.

The Loss of Material Blessings

> *9:1 O Israel, do not rejoice jubilantly like the nations, for you are unfaithful to your God. You love to receive a prostitute's wages on all the floors where you thresh your grain.*

Just like so many people today, Israel rejoiced in the good things of life, such as material prosperity, good friends, good company and good food. Sadly, these things had usurped God's place in the life of the Israelites; they did not rejoice in God. The Lord is jealous for his people's affections, therefore he tells Israel that since she is not delighting in the Lord, her material joys will be taken away from her.

Although she knew the Lord, she had deserted him; all over the country the children of Israel were offering sacrifices to false gods. When the harvest was gathered in, Israel should have celebrated with a feast to the Lord known as Succoth, or the feat of Tabernacles (Lev 23:39–43). She should have given thanks to him and brought him the first fruits of her increase. Instead, she honoured the idols of Baalim and indulged in the pagan rites of that religion. The words "rejoice jubilantly" may imply the riotous, ungodly way in which these rites were carried out, in stark contrast to the holy exuberance of true worship.

> *9:2 Threshing floors and wine vats will not feed the people, and new wine only deceives them.*

So, God would cause their harvests to fail, both of grain and vine, until they learned that it is only God who provided them with all things richly to enjoy (1 Tim 6:17).

> *9:3 They will not remain in the Lord's land. Ephraim will return to Egypt; they will eat ritually unclean food in Assyria.*

God had promised the land to Israel as part of his covenant with them, but since Israel had broken that covenant and no longer wished to walk with God, he would remove her from the land (Deut 28:58–64). The return to Egypt probably symbolised a return to slavery and wanton poverty in the land of Assyria, although it is certainly possible that the Assyrians would have sold some Israelites as slaves to Egypt itself.

The Loss of Spiritual Blessings

> *9:4 They will not pour out drink offerings of wine to the Lord; they will not please him with their sacrifices. Their sacrifices will be like bread eaten while in mourning; all those who eat them will make themselves ritually unclean. For their bread will be only to satisfy their appetite; it will not come into the temple of the Lord.*

Not only would Israel's material blessings be denied, but since she had rejected the spiritual blessings of worshipping the one true God, he would now deprive her of these too. Israel took great pride in the fact that they were God's chosen people, and this relationship was symbolised by Israel's abstention from common or unclean food.

Yet this distinction would be removed, as they would be forced to eat unclean food for survival. The exiles would be unable—not being allowed by their captors—to offer drink offerings to the Lord. Nor would they be able to offer animal sacrifices to him. All the means which Israel had of approaching God and of worshipping him would be taken away, since they had despised them when they had them.

This may also provide a warning for Christians today—those who do not attend church may find one day that when they desperately wish they could attend church there will be no church for them to attend. Those who think little of reading the Bible may find themselves without opportunity to do so in time to come. Let us never take these blessings of God for granted.

For years, they had not brought their tithes and offerings to the house of God, and now in their desperate state, when they wished to bring them, they could not, for the house of God was many miles away and burned with fire. From a very practical point of view, those Christians who neglect fellowship and tithing are putting extreme pressure on both their church and their ministers. The day will come when something will give way— either the minister will be forced out to find work so that he and his family can afford to eat, thus neglecting the more important matter of the word of God, or the church itself will close and then there will be no place set apart locally for divine worship.

Then they will say when the church was there the people didn't care but when it was taken away it was too late. Incidentally, it is far harder to start a church than to keep one going.

> *9:5 So what will you do on the festival day, on the festival days of the Lord?*

The nation's joy was once symbolised by the national observance of the feasts of the Lord. But now in a foreign land, with no temple or priesthood, what were they to do? For generations, Jerusalem was the place where the people gathered to worship Yahweh (2 Chron 33:3), but God had taken away their opportunity to worship him there. The end of these festivals symbolised the end of the nation's joy and the beginning of its mourning.

> *9:6 Look! Even if they flee from the destruction, Egypt will take hold of them, and Memphis will bury them. The weeds will inherit the silver they treasure – thorn bushes will occupy their homes.*

The remains of the nation's former wealth would be carried off by the Egyptians and the dead buried by them. Memphis was the great burial place of the Egyptians, equivalent to a huge cemetery.

In the place where Israel once lived, the land flowing with milk and honey, thorns and thistles would grow, due to the lack of human inhabitants to cultivate the land. This emphasises the desolation brought on as a result of turning from the Lord.

> *9:7 The time of judgment is about to arrive! The time of retribution is imminent! Let Israel know! The prophet is considered a fool–the inspired man is viewed as a madman–because of the multitude of your sins and your intense animosity.*

It was time, says Hosea, for the nation to be punished for its wickedness. The Assyrian invasion threatened by God was not a prediction of the far distant future, but of a day near at hand. Yet the people had ridiculed and mocked the prophets who brought his message, for since they loved sin and darkness they hated to be told the truth.

> *9:8 The prophet is a watchman over Ephraim on behalf of God, yet traps are laid for him along all of his paths; animosity rages against him in the land of his God.*

The prophets were appointed by God to safeguard his people, and the word of God delivered to Israel by them was another example of the spiritual blessings they had spurned. They had paid no attention to his word, but openly hated and despised the prophets and tried to stop them preaching even in the temple of God.

> *9:9 They have sunk deep into corruption as in the days of Gibeah. He will remember their wrongdoing. He will repay them for their sins.*

The Lord compares the people of Hosea's day to those of Gibeah in the days of the Judges. This terrible incident is recorded in Judges 19 & 20. To summarise, the men of Gibeah were every bit as bad as the men of Sodom. The people of Israel knew the story well, for the tribe of Benjamin had been almost entirely wiped out. Just as God did not overlook the sin of Gibeah, so he will not now overlook the sin of Israel but will punish it fully. It is likely that the practices of the men of Gibeah were wide spread in Israel and that a punishment similar to that given to Benjamin would be the result.

> *9:10 When I found Israel, it was like finding grapes in the wilderness. I viewed your ancestors like an early fig on a fig tree in its first season. Then they came to Baal-Peor and they dedicated themselves to shame – they became as detestable as what they loved.*

Why had this decline come about? God reminds Israel of the time when he had first brought her out of Egypt into a relationship with himself. As a man would be delighted, surprised, and refreshed to find early grapes in the desert, so God had delighted in Israel and her love for him. Indeed, some regard the first or white figs to be the best and sweetest fruit known to man, and this symbolised the sweetness of Israel's first love for God. This is how the relationship should have remained, with Israel separated to the Lord. Balaam (Num 22–24), failed to curse Israel; however, he succeeded in bringing about her downfall. This was achieved by instructing the Moabite king Balak to send women to seduce the Israelites to commit sexual immorality and to sacrifice to idols (Num 31:16). It was these Moabite women who had taught the Israeli men the way to worship Baal at the place Peor which is why it was referred to as Baal Peor. The root of the matter was that they had deserted God in favour of Baal and so became as foul as the idols/demons they loved and worshipped. Sadly, this practice was continued even in the New Testament (Rev 2:14). Backsliding begins in the heart that turns away from God, and finds expression in the life lived without God.

The Loss of Children

> *9:11–12 Ephraim will be like a bird; what they value will fly away. They will not bear children – they will not enjoy pregnancy – they will not even conceive! Even if they raise their children, I will take away every last one of them. Woe to them! For I will turn away from them.*

The children of Israel were meant to be the spiritual children of God. They were to love and serve him only. But as they were now brought up to love and serve Baal they had become, spiritually, the children of Baal. This practise had continued for generations and would continue for as long as it remained unchecked. So, God would kill the children born figuratively to Baal. Either they would die at birth or in the womb or they would never be conceived at all. The glory of Israel (AV – "what they value" in NET above) is a reference to her sons, particularly to the number of her children, which God had promised would be as the sand by the seashore innumerable (Gen 22:17). Thus a reduction in population is indicated in these verses. If the babies did survive into early childhood, it would only be to die or taken into captivity, for it would be a bitter thing indeed for the nation when God turned his back on her.

> *9:13 Just as lion cubs are born predators, so Ephraim will bear his sons for slaughter.*

In his vision, Hosea saw that the sons of Israel were doomed, that the fathers would be forced to bring their own sons forward for execution to the enemy, who lurked like lions waiting to devour.

> *9:14 Give them, O Lord – what will you give them? Give them wombs that miscarry, and breasts that cannot nurse!*

So terrible was the prospect, that Hosea, realising that God's purpose was fixed, prayed rather for the women to be barren than for them to bear children who would live to face the horror to come.

Jesus said something similar to the women of his day, as he predicted what would happen to his people at the very end of the age (Luke 23:27–31).

> *9:15 Because of all their evil in Gilgal, I hate them there. On account of their evil deeds, I will drive them out of my land. I will no longer love them; all their rulers are rebels.*

Gilgal was one of the principle centres for Baal worship and it was here that Israel, like an adulterous wife, had proved unfaithful to Jehovah. It was because of this that God would no longer show them special favour. This is what is meant by "I began to hate them." The adulterous wife would no longer be loved as when she was faithful. Israel would be rejected as God's own people and driven from the land of Israel. God would remove the blessings and protection of his being Israel's husband, for even the nation's rulers were rebels against him.

> *9:16 Ephraim will be struck down – their root will be dried up; they will not yield any fruit. Even if they do bear children, I will kill their precious offspring.*

Since Ephraim (Israel) had not brought fruit for God (in fact was so far past being able to do so that she was dead in her root) so God would destroy the fruit which she did produce—the fruit of her womb. At present, there was no hope of restoration for the nation. Indeed, the drastic action of the Assyrian invasion was the only thing which successfully stopped the rot of idolatry in Israel.

> *9:17 My God will reject them, for they have not obeyed him; so they will be fugitives among the nations.*

God would hurl the people out of the promised land, since they were no longer deserving to live there. They had refused to listen to his voice and now they would suffer as fugitives in a foreign land. This prophecy was literally fulfilled in 721 BCE.

Chapter 10:1–15 Impending Doom

Prosperity Led to Apostasy

10:1 Israel was a fertile vine that yielded fruit. As his fruit multiplied, he multiplied altars to Baal. As his land prospered, they adorned the fertility pillars.

The reason Israel was a fruitful vine is that God had planted her in the land, and there had been times in her history when she had brought forth the fruits of righteousness and the worship of God. Isaiah recounts how God brought Israel out of Egypt, using horticultural language to describe how God tended and cared for his people as a gardener cares for his vine in the hope it will produce fruit (see Isa 5). Jesus used similar language concerning God in John 15, but there he identifies himself rather than Israel as the vine through which God's perfect will is expressed. Jesus explained that it is only as Christians are joined to Christ and share his life, that they can produce fruit (John 15:1–8).

Sadly, the fruit of God's blessing, which yielded material prosperity, was a bitter one. Rather than returning thanksgiving to God, and prospering in their spiritual life as in their material life, they gave thanks to the gods and forces of nature by worshipping the idols of the Baalim. As a result, they became an unfruitful vine, which as Ezekiel points out, is god for nothing, since barren vines are not even useful for their wood (Ezek 15:1–5).

10:2 Their heart is slipping; soon they will be punished for their guilt. The LORD will break their altars; he will completely destroy their fertility pillars.

A better rendering would be "they are double-hearted" in the sense that Elijah indicted them (1 Kgs 18:21). That is, although they worshipped the Lord, and his feasts were not entirely abandoned by them, in the northern kingdom the feasts were not kept according to God's commands. Their worship took the form of syncretism—a mixture of their ancestral Old Testament worship and the Canaanite religion of Baal worship. The people served the Lord with the mouths, but even the casual observer of religious life of Israel at that time would identify the chief deity of the nation was Baal. Here the focus of God's action in judgment is seen to be the idol cult; this is the reason for Israel's destruction.

> *10:3 Very soon they will say, "We have no king since we did not fear the LORD. But what can a king do for us anyway?"*

Here the prophet reveals how Israel thought light of the punishment of God on their nation. The king of Israel no longer performed his function as national and to a great extent spiritual leader, and would soon be removed from office, and the kingdom forever ended. At that time the people would say "what use was a king anyway?" On the one hand this may represent the anarchy which prevailed during the reigns of the kings of Israel, so that society moved backward to the days of the judges in which everyone did what was right in his own eyes; yet on the other hand it speaks of the utter despair of a nation at the mercy of its enemies, its king powerless to deliver them from God's anger.

> *10:4 They utter empty words, taking false oaths and making empty agreements. Therefore legal disputes sprout up like poisonous weeds in the furrows of a plowed field.*

Their words are empty, devoid of meaning, having no spiritual or moral quality and so conveying no meaning or guidance or blessing (Mal 2:7; Col 4:6; Tit 1:9). God does not condemn them for taking oaths, but for knowingly taking false oaths. Taking oaths was the practise in legal agreements. For the Israel of Hosea's time, no legal contract was binding; they were prepared to break their word if it profited them. As a result, legal and contractual disputes commonly arose which God here compares to poison destroying the life of the nation.

This is as much a lesson for the Christian church today as it was for the nation of Israel then. There is much talk about unity in the church leading to blessing, however we need to hear God's word about what truly keeps a people together. The key to unity is righteousness; that is, to live in a right relation with God and other people.

The New Testament contains a great deal of practical advice on this subject. Jesus, for instance, warns against the taking of oaths, not in the legal sense but in the sense that we should be known as those who always speak the truth, and whose word can be depended on (Matt 5:34–37). There can be no unity without trust and there can be no trust without honesty where a person keeps their word even though it be to their hurt (Ps 15:4).

> *10:5–6 The inhabitants of Samaria will lament over the calf idol of Beth Aven. Its people will mourn over it; its idolatrous priests will wail over it, because its splendor will be taken from them into exile. Even the calf idol will be carried to Assyria, as tribute for the great king. Ephraim will be disgraced; Israel will be put to shame because of its wooden idol.*

A common theme in the Old Testament is that the outward manifestation of idolatry leads to inward spiritual decline in the life of the individual and of the nation. Psalm 115:8 says that the idol worshipper becomes like his idol—which is to say worthless from a spiritual perspective; without character or virtue. The nation had been led into spiritual decline and God would deal at once with the root cause.

The first step to national idolatry was the setting up of the golden calf at Beth Aven by Jeroboam I (2 Chron 13:8). However, they would no longer be able to worship this idol when it was taken into exile in Assyria as the spoil of war; the cult would be ended once and for all.

The challenge to the Christian then is, what is the root cause of your spiritual decline? Are you letting God deal with it? There will be no progress in your spiritual life until he does. The Christian cannot withhold that part of their heart that God is trying to deal with. True Christian spirituality is characterised by all or nothing commitment.

> *10:7 Samaria and its king will be carried off like a twig on the surface of the waters.*

Here, with reference to verse 3, we see that Samaria (Northern Israel) did indeed still have a king at this time, Hoshea. The Prophet states that Hoshea and his people would be taken into exile by Assyrian forces in a way which the prophet compares to a twig thrown into the river and being swept away.

> *10:8 The high places of the "House of Wickedness" will be destroyed; it is the place where Israel sins. Thorns and thistles will grow up over its altars. Then they will say to the mountains, "Cover us!" and to the hills, "Fall on us!"*

The text gives the name of a place Beth-Aven, which is translated here "House of Wickedness", a major centre of idol worship. Its destruction would end idol worship in the land, and would involve terrible human cost. The altars would be abandoned to thorns and thistles, rather like a disused graveyard, whilst in human terms the violence would be so severe that the people would cry in vain for shelter. The highest mountains or deepest caves could not save them, and in vain they would call for the ground to swallow them. A similar picture is used by Jesus in Luke and in Revelation, again to denote the futility of hiding from the judgment of God. In the first case, by Jesus predicting the destruction of Jerusalem c. 70 CE in Luke 23:28–30; and in the second by John writing of judgment at the end of the world in Rev 6:16–17.

> *10:9 O Israel, you have sinned since the time of Gibeah, and there you have remained. Did not war overtake the evildoers in Gibeah?*

Once again referring to the dark times when the Judges ruled (see Hosea 9:9), God declares that Israel, despite its original outrage at some of the atrocities committed at that time had not changed her ways at all, but was still in the same moral and spiritual situation. The consequence of the sin of Gibeah was the extermination of almost the whole tribe of Benjamin, yet this tragic case was insufficient to act as a warning to turn Israel from her sinful course.

> *10:10 When I please, I will discipline them; I will gather nations together to attack them, to bind them in chains for their two sins.*

As God over his people, Yahweh could and would punish them whenever and however he pleased. The nature of this punishment is again to be at the hands of enemy nations, who would chain them and take them into exile; this is as a consequence of their "two sins". This phrase "two sins" may be a reference to the two calves at Bethel and Dan which led the way in Israel's idolatry. Some commentators think, however, that a farming allusion is intended, in keeping with the following verse (v. 11). When oxen are correctly yoked, they pull together to make one furrow; if any animal refuses to cooperate, two furrows will be the unintended result. The picture here means that Israel was not properly yoked to Yahweh, and so was pulling in its own direction.

> *10:11 Ephraim was a well-trained heifer who loved to thresh grain; I myself put a fine yoke on her neck. I will harness Ephraim. Let Judah plow! Let Jacob break up the unplowed ground for himself!*

Again commentators are divided about the exact meaning of this verse. It is true that since Israel had been unwilling to serve God, they would now be placed in chains and made to serve Assyria. This would occur until they learned the difference between serving God and other masters (2 Chron 12:8). Although God had gently dealt with Israel (Ephraim), blessing and making her burden easy, and her work light, she had refused the yoke of Yahweh. As a consequence, God would now place the hard and bitter yoke of Assyria on her; who would force her to break unploughed ground, a picture of hard labour. This was in direct contrast to God, who had given them fields they had not ploughed or planted (Deut 6:10–11).

It is, however, possible to see God's mention of his gentle kindness and mercy to be still applicable to the current situation. Hence his means of bringing the people to repentance would be kindness (Rom 2:4) and that following affliction he would again restore Israel. Even so, this would necessarily be preceded by the kind of ploughing referred to in v. 12.

Only One Remedy

> *10:12 Sow righteousness for yourselves, reap unfailing love. Break up the unplowed ground for yourselves, for it is time to seek the LORD, until he comes and showers deliverance on you.*

The prophet's call to the people as a remedy for this situation is not for an outward show of religion, but for inward reformation of the heart produced by genuine repentance. Once again, farming analogies are used. A farmer must first break up the unploughed ground before sowing his seed. Israel must be possessed of a broken and contrite spirit, expressing sorrow for sin if their hearts are to be cleansed. Ploughing is necessary to prepare the ground to receive the sown seed, and also for removing weeds and thorns which are already in the soil. In the case of Israel, it is a reference to the removal of idolatry and other corrupt affections and lusts. By keeping the commandments of the Lord they would be sowing to themselves in righteousness; a thought similar to that which Paul uses when he tells believers to sow to the Spirit (Gal 6:7–8). The benefit they would reap would be the mercy of God. Yet it is not mercy but the source of mercy who needs to be sought; they must seek the Lord. The same is true for today we must seek the Lord if we would know that aspect of revival which involves the setting of ourselves right with God. Once again God describes this blessing in arable terms, as abundant rain which softens the ground and produces a harvest. God's mercy is abundant, and it is that mercy which the church needs today; a heart-softening shower of divine mercy to bring us to the place where we will walk in the right way with God and receive abundant blessing in our individual and church lives.

> *10:13 But you have plowed wickedness; you have reaped injustice; you have eaten the fruit of deception. Because you have depended on your chariots; you have relied on your many warriors.*

Tragically, when faced with disaster at the hands of the approaching Assyrian armies, Israel did not accept God's offer of mercy, for they did not like the terms which it involved (turning from sin). Instead King Hoshea sought the help of the King of Egypt, and looked for a military solution to the problem. Since the nation's problem was its sin, and the judgement it faced came from God, any thought of avoiding it by natural means was vain. One cannot hope to run and hide from God whether one is a sinner fleeing his wrath or a child of God fleeing his will and purpose for their lives, as Jonah found out.

> *10:14–15 The roar of battle will rise against your people; all your fortresses will be devastated, just as Shalman devastated Beth Arbel on the day of battle, when mothers were dashed to the ground with their children. So will it happen to you, O Bethel, because of your great wickedness! When that day dawns, the king of Israel will be destroyed.*

The prophet reiterates God's unambiguous message that the oncoming battle would spell doom for the nation. Since they had trusted in armaments, these would be of no use to them, and the cities named are representative of what would happen to the entire kingdom, to mothers, children and to the King. Notice that God himself is not here voicing that he will kill anyone, but rather that as a result of Israel's sin he would allow the cruel Assyrians to come, and without his protection, they would deal with Israel as if they were any other nation. The reality for Israel is that they had fallen so low, that they could no longer expect the miraculous deliverance of Yahweh.

Chapter 11:1–12:1 Israel's Unfaithfulness

God's Unchanging Love

> *11:1 When Israel was a young man, I loved him like a son, and I summoned my son out of Egypt.*

God looks back with the yearning love of a parent whose child has gone astray. He remembers the time when he adopted the nation of Israel to be his own people, and loved them as a father loves his son. With the call to become God's sons came the call to serve God, and this was the reason for the Exodus, the summoning out of Egypt—"let my people go *that they might serve me*" *(Exod 7:16)*.

This idea was also applied by Matthew to the Lord Jesus Christ who following his childhood exile in Egypt returned to Israel to be the servant and son of God (Matt 2:15).

> *11:2 But the more I summoned them, the farther they departed from me. They sacrificed to the Baal idols and burned incense to images.*

Yet from the very beginning of God's relationship with the nation they had been unfaithful to him and to his call (Exod 32:4). Once again during the time of Hosea they had departed from God to offer sacrifices and incense as part of their worship to the Baal idols. The idolatry which revealed itself in the golden calf incident was not a one-off failing.

> *11:3 Yet it was I who led Ephraim, I took them by the arm; but they did not acknowledge that I had healed them.*

God's kindness to the people here is compared to that of a parent helping a child learn to walk. Despite God's loving-kindness in leading them out of Egypt, giving them his blessings, laws, and the spiritual means of approaching God in worship, the people did not acknowledge God or thank him for his goodness. This is all the more surprising when one considers the level of supernatural activity which God exerted on their behalf at that time. The reference to God being the one who healed them may be an allusion to God's miraculous acts of healing the people when they were sick (Exo 15:26; Num 12:13), as well as to the exodus—the act which made the nation whole.

> *11:4 I led them with leather cords, with leather ropes; I lifted the yoke from their neck, and gently fed them.*

Changing the analogy, God describes his dealings with Israel as being like those of a farmer caring for his livestock. His people were not like animals who were led by a bit between the teeth or by hooks through the nose. God likens them instead to animals wearing well-fitting harnesses which would not chafe the skin.

The picture is that of a kind livestock owner. God's treatment of the people was always kind and considerate; he led them with skill. God's mastery did not mean a heavy yoke for them, such as they had known in their slavery in Egypt, and it is an understanding of this which underpins Jesus's analogy of his own yoke being easy and his burden light (Matt 11:30). Furthermore, they were not like half-starved animals labouring under hard conditions, but like those who were well fed.

God stooped to feed his people quite literally with manna from heaven (Exod 16:12). Yet he fed them with much more than this, for by becoming God's covenant people they ate of the spiritual food and drank of the spiritual drink which their journeys prefigured, the promise of a new covenant in Christ (1 Cor 10:3–4).

Israel's Slavery

> *11:5 They will return to Egypt! Assyria will rule over them because they refuse to repent!*

The people had rejected God and his purpose for them to such an extent that they sought to make a military alliance with Egypt, the land from which God had delivered them (2 Kgs 17:4). They would figuratively return to Egypt, by once again becoming slaves. It is not clear whether some Jews actually thought that by escaping to Egypt they would be safe from the Assyrians. If so, after the fall of Egypt to Assyria, this hope was dashed. If only they would repent and return to God could they be saved, but since they preferred idolatry to the service of God, they would go into exile as slaves to the Assyrians.

> *11:6–7 A sword will flash in their cities, it will destroy the bars of their city gates, and will devour them in their fortresses. My people are obsessed with turning away from me to Baal, but he will never exalt them!*

The violence of war is depicted here as the means by which the nation would fall. Critics of God call to attention the violent way in which his judgment fell upon the people. Those who are not blinded by such prejudice see clearly, as Hosea does, that the yearning heart of God was desperate to avoid this tragedy. Despite all of his attempts to avert judgment, the people continued to turn to idols, and they could find no salvation or blessing in this direction.

God does not wish any sinner to perish or to face his judgement (1 Tim 2:4; 2 Pet 3:9). The lengths he has gone to in order to avoid such a disaster are great indeed—the agonising death of his only begotten son as a substitute for sinners. Yet people still reject this God-given way of salvation, rushing headlong for disaster. Therefore, it must be recognised that God took the initiative in the plan of salvation and that there is hope for all who will come to God through Christ.

Israel's Future Restoration the Result of God's Love

> *11:8 How can I give you up, O Ephraim? How can I surrender you, O Israel? How can I treat you like Admah? How can I make you like Zeboiim? I have had a change of heart! All my tender compassions are aroused!*

Here one hears the heart cry of God, as Hosea returns to the theme of the opening verses where he described Israel as a son. Even if he could give up another, yet he could not give up his own people. God's glory and covenants had been bound up with Israel and her ancestors (Rom 9:4–5). He could not treat her as any other nation. Moses had understood this, which is why he was able to turn God away from the fierceness of his anger (Exod 32:11–14). In the absence of Moses, God's own heart intercedes for the people, moving himself to compassion and action.

In the same way, it was while we were without strength and unworthy that God sent his own son. God intervened in human affairs by his own volition because there was no other intercessor (Isa 59:16; Rom 5:8). It is because of Christ's intervention that even sinners are at this time surrounded by the mercy of God. However, this mercy will not be offered to the unrepentant forever, which is why we must repent of our sin and accept Christ as savour while the opportunity remains (2 Cor 6:2).

> *11:9 I cannot carry out my fierce anger! I cannot totally destroy Ephraim! Because I am God, and not man — the Holy One among you —I will not come in wrath!*

It is because of his divine nature, "I am God, and not man", that God decided that even though the punishment of Israel would be severe it would not be terminal. If God's anger in the deportation of Israel into slavery was tempered, what would his full wrath look like? Yet because of God's mercy Israel would not be utterly destroyed or cast off as a people.

11:10–11 He will roar like a lion, and they will follow the LORD; when he roars, his children will come trembling from the west. They will return in fear and trembling like birds from Egypt, like doves from Assyria, and I will settle them in their homes," declares the LORD.

Here is God's promise of a return for Israel, a return to the promised land for the northern kingdom.[13] In fear of God, with regard to his holiness and his actions they would be permitted to return like migrating birds return to their home. This is a picture of their exile being temporary, and perhaps indicative of God's covenant love for Israel extending into the present time; in view of the modern day return of Israel to its ancestral homeland.

11:12–12:1 Ephraim has surrounded me with lies; the house of Israel has surrounded me with deceit. But Judah still roams about with God; he remains faithful to the Holy One.

The first fruit or token of God's unfailing purpose towards his people would be Judah, who at Hosea's time of writing remained faithful to God and walked in his ways. Although later they sinned and were exiled to Babylon, within 70 years their repentance brought them back to God, and they returned from exile to remain in their land for hundreds of years (Ezek 28:25) prior to the Roman wars with Judea.

---

[13] Note the direction of the return, for Israel was initially scattered eastward, so God's language is deliberately inclusive—so much so that some commentators have even seen an allusion here to the words of Jesus (Matt 8:11).

Chapter 12:1–14 Feeding on the Wind

12:1 Ephraim continually feeds on the wind; he chases the east wind all day; he multiplies lies and violence. They make treaties with Assyria, and send olive oil as tribute to Egypt.

The emptiness of Israel's spiritual experience is here emphasised. The words used to denote feeding and chasing (or seeking) are words which should have applied to the nation's relationship with God. God had told his people to partake of or feed on him, and to seek him with their whole heart, and in this way they would find him and be spiritually filled and satisfied. Indeed, no other temporal blessing, however great, can make up for the absence of spiritual blessing in one's life. These principles are further developed in the Old Testament: feeding upon God, Ps 63:5; Isa 55:2; Jer 31:14; seeking God, Ps 119:10; Jer 29:13; Amos 5:4.

Jesus continued this important theme in John 6:27, when he called his followers not to "work for the food that disappears, but for the food that remains to eternal life — the food which the Son of Man will give to you". He continued his instruction by calling us instead to "seek first the kingdom of God and his righteousness" (Matt 6:33 ESV). Paul affirms this necessity when he urges the Colossians to "seek the things that are above, where Christ is, seated at the right hand of God" (Col 3:1).

However, Israel (Ephraim here is a synonym for Israel) were seeking Baal rather than God, an exercise which God compares to feeding on thin air. They wore themselves out eagerly serving Baal, but it did not benefit them at all. The east wind is scorching, damaging to crops (e.g. Gen 41:6), and in this way Hosea describes how Israel's preoccupation with Baal did nothing but harm. Idols are nothing (e.g. Isa 37:18), but the spiritual powers behind them are genuine (1 Cor 10:19–20; Eph 6:12); even so, all they can offer are empty carnal experiences, what Paul describes as the weak and beggarly elements of the world, the kind of empty lifestyle which appealed to the Galatians (Gal 4:9).

At the same time the people of Israel devoted themselves to breaking God's commandments, proving themselves to be his enemies. The emptiness of spiritual life leads to corruption of moral life and the disintegration of the social and community life of the nation. As a result, when disaster loomed, the people had no relationship with God, and so there was no calling on the Lord for deliverance. Instead, they gave gifts to appease the Assyrians and made military pacts with the Egyptians for protection but all to no avail. As in the personal realm so in the national, without God to rely on, one is dependent on nothing but hot air.

> *12:2 The LORD also has a covenant lawsuit against Judah; he will punish Jacob according to his ways and repay him according to his deeds.*

God had made Israel his own people, revealing himself to them by his name the LORD (which he had not previously Exod 6:3), and brought them into covenant at Sinai. This covenant contained blessings for obedience but also pronounced curses or judgments for disobedience. Since Israel was his covenant people, and they had broken his covenant, they would be judged and punished according to all which that covenant pronounced (see Deut 28:15–68).

> *12:3–5 In the womb he attacked his brother; in his manly vigor he struggled with God. He struggled with an angel and prevailed; he wept and begged for his favor. He found God at Bethel, and there he spoke with him! As for the LORD God Almighty, the LORD is the name by which he is remembered!*

This allusion to the founder of the nation—Jacob, whose name was changed by God to Israel— is applied to Hosea's present-day situation in both a positive and negative sense. From a negative point of view, Jacob had been a deceiver, one who broke covenant bonds with his closest family, just as Israel now broke the covenant bonds of its relationship with Yahweh. As a man he struggled to submit to God's will and purpose for his life. Yet at Peniel, by eventually humbling himself to yield to God with bitter tears and pleadings, he became a changed man. Having been broken by his experience he was now willing to surrender his life to any course which the Lord had planned. This is why God granted him a blessing at Peniel, speaking directly to him and removing the stigma of his former name (Jacob means deceiver), re-naming him Israel (a prince with God)—see Gen 32:24-32.

The positive application of this lesson is clear, for if Jacob the covenant breaker could be restored and renewed then so could the nation which bore his name. Verse 5 illustrates that the Lord has not changed, he still bears his covenant keeping name and will show the same love and grace to Israel if he were sought.

> *12:6 But you must return to your God, by maintaining love and justice, and by waiting for your God to return to you.*

Here the promise of restoration is revealed: if the people return to their God he too will certainly return to be their God. If only they will seek him he will be found by them and he would be willing to have mercy on them. Yet they must seek him whilst grace is still being offered (Isa 55:6). They must seek him earnestly with all their heart (Jer 29:13) and sincerely. This must not be merely an outward show of religion, but one which reveals evidence of a changed heart in terms of love (faithfulness to God and his covenant) and justice (exhibiting the loving virtues of that covenant with other people).

In the NT John the Baptist insisted that such fruits of repentance should be produced by those with genuine religion (Luke 3:8), as did Jesus (John 15:2). Paul further expands on what this means for believers in 2 Cor 5:17 and Gal 5:20-22, as well as his many practical exhortations about change in the life of a truly repentant person (e.g. 1 Cor 6:9-11; Eph 4:28).

> *12:7–8 The businessmen love to cheat; they use dishonest scales. Ephraim boasts, "I am very rich! I have become wealthy! In all that I have done to gain my wealth, no one can accuse me of any offense that is actually sinful."*

Of all the sins of Israel, its idolatry and the breakdown of society and law and order leading to violence, one may wonder why God highlights here the sins of dishonesty and avarice; but these are indeed deadly sins. In a society which turns its back upon God, selfishness and dishonesty reign in business, the only aim of which is to get rich quick. The reason for God's interest is that this means getting rich at the expense of the poor, who live off the land and who can ill-afford to be cheated of even the smallest amounts. God is the defender of the poor and of those on the margins of society, such as widows and orphans, who do not have the privileges others have. Be warned that when no one speaks up on their behalf, and no one does what it right on their behalf, God himself will take action and he will hold those guilty who trample on the poor (Amos 5:11; Isa 10:1–2).

Israel's sin was compounded by their hard-hearted refusal to acknowledge their misdemeanours. It is always the case that the penitent will find mercy from God (Isa 55:7) whereas the impenitent will instead face wrath (Zech 7:11–12; Rom 2:5).

> *12:9 "I am the LORD your God who brought you out of Egypt; I will make you live in tents again as in the days of old.*

The terms of the covenant are again invoked, to remind the nation of its shortcomings and yet of God's faithfulness. At the exodus, Israel dwelt in tents as they were rescued from slavery. Tragically, in the deportation they would once more dwell in tents as they were taken back into slavery—how far they must have fallen from grace!

> *12:10 I spoke to the prophets; I myself revealed many visions; I spoke in parables through the prophets."*

This tragic event in Israel's history would happen in spite of Gods faithfulness. He had sent his messages to warn, rebuke and exhort the people through his prophets and by the visions which he gave to them. The sentiment of 11:1 and 12:6 is again coming through: if only they had listened!

> *12:11 Is there idolatry in Gilead? Certainly its inhabitants will come to nothing! Do they sacrifice bulls in Gilgal? Surely their altars will be like stones heaped up on a plowed field!*

Gilead was to the east of the Jordan just within Israel's border and Gilgal to the west of the Jordan. This phrase is meant to be indicative of the whole nation becoming worthless through its complete embracing of idol worship. God would visit them with judgment by breaking down the altars on which sacrifices were made to idols.

> *12:12-13 Jacob fled to the country of Aram, then Israel worked to acquire a wife; he tended sheep to pay for her. The LORD brought Israel out of Egypt by a prophet, and due to a prophet Israel was preserved alive.*

Just as God preserved Jacob when he went to Aram (modern day Syria) to find a wife (Gen 28), so he preserved Israel as he brought her out of Egypt. Here is a picture of Israel becoming Yahweh's wife or covenant partner. Obtaining a wife cost Jacob dearly and God would remind his people of what it has cost him to make Israel his own. At that time, he had sent a prophet to bring them out of Egypt, but the people were now rejecting the prophets which God had sent to them, effectively repudiating their covenant relationship with Yahweh.

12:14 But Ephraim bitterly provoked him to anger; so he will hold him accountable for the blood he has shed, his Lord will repay him for the contempt he has shown.

Hosea describes this deliberate rejection of the prophetic word as revealing contempt for God, something which directly provoked God's anger. They were rebels who trampled his covenant faithfulness underfoot, and they would be punished accordingly.

Even in the New Testament, a warning is given for those who despise and reject God's covenant goodness having initially chosen to accept its terms (see Heb 10:28–31; 12:25).

Chapter 13:1–16 No Deliverance

Israel's Pride led to its Destruction

> *13:1 When Ephraim spoke, trembling, He exalted himself in Israel; But when he offended through Baal worship, he died. (NKJV™)*

I have chosen the NKJV "when Israel spoke with trembling" rather than the NET "when Israel spoke there was terror" because it makes better sense in the context. A holy trembling at the awesomeness of God is implied, worship characterised by deep reverence for God.

When Israel walked in the fear of God he was exalted as a true "prince with God" (the meaning of "Israel"). However, the same nation or even the same person who has been exalted by being a true worshipper of God may even then fall from grace. Ephraim turned to idols, and this is what brought about his destruction (Heb 6:4–6; 2 Pet 3:17).

> *13:2 Now they sin more and more, And have made for themselves molded images, Idols of their silver, according to their skill; All of it is the work of craftsmen. They say of them, "Let the men who sacrifice kiss the calves!" (NKJV™)*

At the time of the prophet's message, when God had appealed to them and warned them of the consequences of their sin, they continued to defy him. Further to the introduction of national idols by Jeroboam, the people were now making their own private idols, the work of men's hands, and adhering to pagan religion. They urged each other on to pagan worship—the phrase "Let the men who sacrifice kiss the calves" could be paraphrased as an instruction to others: "Sacrifice to them (the idols), worship the (golden) calves!"[14] In spiritual terms the Psalmist says that idol worshippers become like their idols, in as much as they are dumb, blind, and useless (Ps 115:4–8).

> *13:3 Therefore they will disappear like the morning mist, like early morning dew that evaporates, like chaff that is blown away from a threshing floor, like smoke that disappears through an open window.*

Because of its sin Israel would be removed from the land as swiftly and as fully as when the morning mist and dew evaporates before the rising sun, as chaff in the wind or as the smoke from a fire vanishes.

> *13:4 But I am the LORD your God, who brought you out of Egypt. Therefore, you must not acknowledge any God but me; except me there is no Savior.*

In contrast with the passing glory of Israel expressed in v. 3, and indeed of all humanity, God's glory is everlasting. His eternal nature and power have been revealed to the nation in the way he brought them out of Egypt and made them his own people. This relationship Israel had with God was unique; it was not shared with any other people. So even if the nations of the world ran after idols, Israel should never have followed their example. Having been saved by the Lord from slavery, they should have acknowledged him as their only God and their only Saviour.

> *13:5 I cared for you in the wilderness, in the dry desert where no water was.*

God once again reminds the people of the defining moment in their history when, as he led them from Egypt through the desert to become a nation. The biblical narrative highlights that this was in order to avoid a situation where they would face war without being ready for it (Exod 13:17–18). God

---

[14] Good News Translation in Today's English Version- Second Edition Copyright © 1992 by American Bible Society. Used by Permission.

was fully aware of the supplies they needed to survive in the wilderness, and so he gave them water from the hard rock and manna from heaven to eat (Neh 9:15).

> *13:6 When they were fed, they became satisfied; when they were satisfied, they became proud; as a result, they forgot me!*

Whilst the people depended on God for their every need, their relationship with Yahweh was strong. However, when the people had plenty and were satisfied, they came to believe they had no more need of God. This independence led them to pride through which they "forgot God"; which is to say, they no longer required him or his services.

> *13:7–9 So I will pounce on them like a lion; like a leopard I will lurk by the path. I will attack them like a bear robbed of her cubs—I will rip open their chests. I will devour them there like a lion—like a wild animal would tear them apart. I will destroy you, O Israel! Who is there to help you?*

Here God speaks of his anger and jealousy. Like a bear robbed of her cubs, so God had been robbed of his people, and the culprits would be torn into pieces as if by wild animals such as the lion and leopard. Since God was the only one who could deliver them, what would happen when it was God who was fighting against them?

> *13:10 Where then is your king, that he may save you in all your cities? Where are your rulers for whom you asked, saying, "Give me a king and princes"?*

The rot which had led the nation away from God had commenced a long time before Jeroboam. It had begun in the desert, when God delivered them from slavery in Egypt, and was certainly a defining feature of the days of the Judges. It was at that time that Israel rejected God as being direct ruler over them, and asked Samuel to appoint a king for them so that they might be like other nations. Again, the important issue to be noted here is their rejection of God (1 Sam 8:4–8).

> *13:11–12 I granted you a king in my anger, and I will take him away in my wrath! The punishment of Ephraim has been decreed; his punishment is being stored up for the future.*

Israel knew their history well, and God reminds them that when they had previously rejected him as ruler, he gave them Saul son of Kish to be their King, but soon destroyed him. This time it would be the nation as a whole, and its present rulers, who were to be destroyed. Tatford states that the reference to Ephraim's punishment being stored up is an allusion to the practise of keeping records of important events: "The documents were tied together and then stored in a depository for safe keeping" (Deut 32:34; Isa 8:16).[15] Of course, the only "depository" God requires is that of his own omniscience. God knows all things, and will call all people to account for all their thoughts, words, and actions. This is a sobering thought for our present generation as well as for the Israel of Hosea's time (Matt 12:36; Rev 20:12). In Israel's case, and perhaps in ours, the future referred to was not the distant future. For Israel the Assyrian invasion would soon take place, and the day of our death and subsequent judgement can occur at any time (Heb 9:27).

> *13:13 The labor pains of a woman will overtake him, but the baby will lack wisdom; when the time arrives, he will not come out of the womb!*

The imagery of a woman going into labour pains is frequently used in the Bible to denote trouble and anguish, especially that which comes suddenly and which is unavoidable (see for example 1 Thess 5:3). Usually, however, when a woman goes into labour her sorrow is short-lived, for in the words of Jesus "she forgets her sorrow because a man child is born into the world" (John 16:21). In Israel's case however, as in the case of a stillborn infant, there would be no comfort after trouble—only more sorrow and heartache.

---

[15] Tatford, Hosea, 159. This is a perfectly valid point, although Dearman notes that the words are more frequently used to refer to pregnancy—so one might say Israel's judgment was "pregnant", i.e. waiting to be delivered.

In nature, of course, no child is ever thought to be responsible for preventing his or her own birth. Yet the clever device of describing the child in this instance as being unwise demonstrates that in Israel's case, this tragedy might have been prevented—they had brought it on themselves.

No Deliverance from Death

> *13:14 Will I deliver them from the power of Sheol? No, I will not! Will I redeem them from death? No, I will not! O Death, bring on your plagues! O Sheol, bring on your destruction! My eyes will not show any compassion!*

This is a difficult verse. The opening words can be read either as statements or questions, although the context favours the latter. However, it is important to note that the negative answers to these questions are implied by the context and are not explicit in the text itself. According to this rendering the meaning of the verse becomes clear: God would not rescue his unrepentant people from coming judgment.

Paul's use of this text in 1 Cor 15:55 is influenced by Isa 25:8. If during Hosea's time, death was to claim the sinful, Isaiah had foreseen a future time when God would ransom sinners from the power of death. Thus Paul uses this text to state the opposite of what is being proposed by Hosea. For Paul, the God who on this occasion refuses to ransom the participants of the first covenant from death nevertheless announces a general promise to deliver from death all who participate in the new covenant in Christ. This deliverance has now been brought powerfully into view through Christ's death and resurrection. It is Christ alone who delivers from the wrath of God and punishment, for he has delivered us from our sin. The implications of this deliverance is that the wages of sin—death—has no hold over the believer. The power of death grappled with Jesus, but he overcame it and by rising again from the dead, he has given every believer final assurance of salvation to eternal life. Thus what Adam lost in the garden (Rom 5:12) and Israel lost through disobedience (Deut 27:26) is restored collectively to that company of people who are believers in Christ. In 1 Cor 15 Paul uses these verses to point ahead to a time when believers will share in the resurrection to eternal life. As a consequence of this eternal life, the body of the believer shall no longer be mortal (subject to death) or corruptible (subject to decay)—see especially 1 Cor 15:51–57.

> *13:15–16 Even though he flourishes like a reed plant, a scorching east wind will come, a wind from the LORD rising up from the desert. As a result, his spring will dry up; his well will become dry. That wind will spoil all his delightful foods in the containers in his storehouse. Samaria will be held guilty, because she rebelled against her God. They will fall by the sword, their infants will be dashed to the ground—their pregnant women will be ripped open.*

Hosea further says that even if Israel appears strong and virile, yet the scorching east wind—the Assyrian army—will come and utterly destroy him and his supplies. Even women and children would be caught up in the tragedy which was occasioned by the people's rebellion against God.

Chapter 14:1-9 The Promise of Future Hope

14:1 Return, O Israel, to the LORD your God, for your sin has been your downfall!

The Lord once again appeals to Israel on the basis of his love, offering them an opportunity for repentance and forgiveness. The nation's downfall was not due to foreign invasion or to failure in military or economic policy, but rather to national sin and rejection of God. God's message through Hosea is that in spite of this, he remained willing to be associated with them; he is the Lord *their* God, and so the door remains open for them to return. There is always hope for the truly repentant (Luke 15:21-24).

14:2 Return to the LORD and repent! Say to him: "Completely forgive our iniquity; accept our penitential prayer, that we may offer the praise of our lips as sacrificial bulls.

God calls for the nation's return to be along clear and simple lines. Clear so that none may mistake them and simple so that none would find them too difficult. Repentance is a spiritual matter, as is prayer. Prayer involves language, a verbalising of what is in the heart. When the people repent, they are to come before God with sincere prayer on their lips. This is more important than the religious ritual of bringing sacrifices, and centres on asking God to forgive their sins, and to accept their prayers and praises. Here we have evidence in the OT that the NT understanding of "the blood of bulls and goats" being unable to take away sins (Heb 10:4) was already appreciated. Such an understanding, that the sacrificial system was without worth if not accompanied by sincerity of heart and repentance toward God, was certainly shared by the author of Psalm 51:16-17.

> *14:3 Assyria cannot save us; we will not ride warhorses. We will never again say, 'Our gods' to what our own hands have made. For only you will show compassion to Orphan Israel!"*

The prayer continues with a confession of faith and trust in God and his action on behalf of his people: "Assyria cannot save us; we will not ride on warhorses." Furthermore, there is the confession of consecration to the Lord and separation from the cult of Baal: "We will never again say 'our gods' to what our hands have made." The reason for this separation and renewed obedience was the fact that only God loved and showed compassion to his erring and helpless people.

The similarities between the message of Hosea and that of the NT are evident, and the pattern or structure of the means of repentance remains consistent, albeit in the NT Christ is the centre of the formula rather than God. The repentant come with honest and sincere prayer which expresses genuine faith. This faith in God is based on his saving action in Christ on behalf of his people, who raised Christ from death for our justification (Rom 4:25). Our confession of consecration to Christ involves the confession of Jesus as Lord accompanied by our faith in his resurrection (Rom 10:9).

Separation from false religious cults was compulsory in the early church, with Luke recording how those who had practised black arts burned their magic paraphernalia. In Acts 19:19 Luke records items with a street value of over 50,000 silver pieces went up in flames in response to conversion to Christ by some at Ephesus. Paul similarly insists that those who confess Christ and who partake in communion should not at the same time be involved in the worship of idols (1 Cor 10:21). Another similarity between Hosea's message and that of the NT is that the reason for the Christian's renewed obedience is the love of God revealed to an erring and helpless humanity: "for while we were yet without strength, Christ died for the ungodly" (Rom 5:6).

14:4 "I will heal their waywardness and love them freely, for my anger will turn away from them.

The result of the sinner returning to God is thought of in the same terms in both the Old and New Testaments. God receives the sinner who is repentant, and also the sinful nation which returns to him. God would restore the fortunes of the nation, renewing his blessings to them ("my anger will turn away from them"). As a result of repentance, the curses which resulted from covenant breaking can be reversed and replaced by the blessings intended for those who keep the covenant (see Deut 28). The forgiveness of God completely removes the sin for which the nation faced wrath, so that it might receive blessing. For the Christian, this turning away from his anger is explained in terms of the cross. It is Jesus's propitiatory sacrifice (a sacrifice that turns away wrath) that makes it possible for the penitent believer in Christ to be cleansed from sin (1 John 2:2).

Not only is cleansing from the guilt of past sin promised. The words "heal their waywardness" signify a fundamental change in the hearts and lives of God's people as the result of repentance. Once again, this sentiment is expressed in the OT in various places; for example, the Psalmist writes of being restored to walk in paths of righteousness (Ps 23:3). In the NT, this is taken as a fulfilment of the OT promise to "write my laws in their minds and on their hearts" (Heb 8:8–12; Jer 31:33–34). It is the born again experience (John 3:3) that cleanses the life in this way making all things new (Tit 3:5; 2 Cor 5:17). Thus truth is also expressed by John when he writes for Christians who sin, but who penitently confess their sins: "he is faithful and just to forgive us our sins and cleanse us from all unrighteousness" (1 John 1:9). The forgiveness deals with the guilt of sin, but cleansing from all unrighteousness frees us from its power, that we may once again walk in righteousness.

14:5 I will be like the dew to Israel; he will blossom like a lily, he will send down his roots like a cedar of Lebanon.

Israel, in its backslidden state, had been pictured as a dry and barren land. However, with its restoration would come what Peter called "times of refreshing from the presence of the Lord" (Acts 3:19). When the dew comes early on the Middle Eastern ground, it brings life, refreshing, and renewing what was barren and parched. Hence the meaning here concerns the spiritual restoration of the nation of Israel. No doubt Peter's use of this illustration on the Day of Pentecost signifies that he understood the message of salvation through Jesus the Messiah to be God's ultimate means of restoring his people. Moreover, he saw the coming of the Holy Spirit to be the fulfilment of the promise to "be as the dew" to his people.

The result of the spiritual renewal of the nation is the restoration of beauty and strength; the beauty of holiness (1 Chron 16:29; 2 Chron 20:21; Ps 29:2; Ps 96:9) and the strength of loyalty to God (see Josh 1). For the Christian, true spiritual beauty (signified by the lily blossom) is seen when the nature of Christ is visibly reproduced in our lives. Similarly, spiritual strength (signified by the cedar of Lebanon) is found when our lives are rooted in Christ and his teaching (Col 2:6–7).

14:6 His young shoots will grow; his splendor will be like an olive tree, his fragrance like a cedar of Lebanon.

"His young shoots will grow" is an expression of new life. Think back to the time you first came to know Jesus Christ as your Lord and Saviour. Everything was new; your new found love for Christ blossomed and resulted in acts of faith and service which you would never have previously considered to be important to your life. This was the same kind of first love he spoke of when he first redeemed Israel, the love he wished to see restored in his people. Once again the NT concept is strikingly similar. The first love we had when we first came to know the Lord is what he wants to be restored in our lives as Christians (Rev 2:4–5).

His splendour will be like an olive tree. The splendour of the olive tree is its produce, its fruit. It is one thing to be beautiful and another to be useful. It is one thing to worship God and another thing to serve God, but both are equally necessary; and both would be the result in the life of restored Israel, just as both should be evident in the life of the Christian. Worship and service are marks of sincerity, and this truth of heart is compared to the beautiful fragrance of the cedar tree. Even the perfect and sincere life of Christ was offered up as a "sacrifice of sweet smell", that is to say, it was pleasing to God (Eph 5:2). It is interesting to note that Paul uses the language of a sweet smelling aroma to describe the gifts sent to him by the Philippian church, meaning that they were acceptable and pleasing to God as a genuine practical expression of their sincere faith (Phil 4:18).

14:7 People will reside again in his shade; they will plant and harvest grain in abundance. They will blossom like a vine, and his fame will be like the wine from Lebanon.

Once again, it is one thing to be beautiful and another to be useful. Israel's service would not be such that had only heavenly application but was of no earthly use. The Bible knows nothing of such a powerless piety, either in the New or Old Testaments. When Israel's commitment to God was restored, being expressed in its worship and service, so people would gather, rallying to the flag of a nation that was right with God (Zech 8:23). The social and political ramifications of a nation turning to God are incalculable, and all of them are positive. Peace along with social and political stability are among these consequences of renewal. A safe and stable society is where all rational people would wish to live ("people will reside again in its shade"). Economic and material prosperity was another beneficial result ("they will plant and harvest grain in abundance"). The fruit of the vine is a common scriptural picture of divine blessing and joy. So abundant would be the blessing of a restored people that the prophet here compares it to the best wine (which came from Lebanon). One may well say that since the fulfilment of all divine blessings upon Israel are to be found in the ministry of Jesus the Messiah, then surely this picture of joy and abundance (spiritual and material) should be expected in our lives (John 10:10; 3 John 1:2). The ministry of the Holy Spirit in the life of the church is thought by some to be expressed in terms of new wine (Luke 5:37–39).

> *14:8 O Ephraim, I do not want to have anything to do with idols anymore! I will answer him and care for him. I am like a luxuriant cypress tree; your fruitfulness comes from me!*

Israel would throw its idols away as a result of returning to the Lord. It is of note that idolatry itself has been largely absent from Jewish culture since the deportation, exile, and return of the people. God would again fulfil his role as the nation's God (as is expressed by the terms "I will answer him and care for him"). God himself would be to them like a tree of life, as the presence of God filling the nation would be like the life in a tree producing its fruit. Of particular relevance here are the fruits of righteousness which are produced within the individual or nation to the glory and praise of God. It is interesting to see these same sentiments in the NT: the fruits of righteousness through Jesus Christ are the work or fruit of the Holy Spirit residing in each believer and in the community collectively (Gal 5:22–23; Phil 1:11).

> *14:9 Who is wise? Let him discern these things! Who is discerning? Let him understand them! For the ways of the LORD are right; the godly walk in them, but in them the rebellious stumble.*

Those who are wise are those who are instructed by the word of God, who know God and his ways (2 Tim 3:15). The verse makes particular reference here to the ways of God in dealing with his people to grant repentance, forgiveness, and mercy. The grace of God, his underserved favour resulting in undeserved blessing, and the way in which it has been demonstrated to humanity through Christ, is described in the NT as revealing to all people (and even angels) the manifold wisdom of God (Eph 3:10). Only the wise and discerning heart can see that it is through revealing his love that God reveals his nature (for God is love—1 John 4:8). It is in his mercy to sinners, rather than in his mighty judgments, that God brings to himself eternal glory (Eph 1:3–6).

Whatever people may think of God's gracious forgiveness and restoration; his way is right. One may consider how even though Israel had strayed far from God, his promise to restore them is "righteous" because he had not abandoned his faithfulness to them. Furthermore, he would not contemplate breaking his promise to them, even if they had abandoned their faithfulness to him. For the Christian, who would count him or herself among the godly, we may consider how God has made atonement for sin so that his justification of the sinner might have a foundation which is sure and righteous (Rom 3:24–26). So we are able to walk securely in the way of salvation.

Yet, how tragic that in Hosea's day (as is still the case today), there were those who were rebellious and who refused to repent and receive God's mercy, thus excluding themselves from the promise of blessing. The rejection of God's mercy in Christ is the theme of numerous prophets, but perhaps especially Isaiah who describes the coming Messiah as "a stone that makes a person trip, and a rock that makes one stumble" (Isa 8:14; see Rom 9:33), especially in terms of Israel's rejection of him. Yet this picture of stumbling is applied by Peter to all—not just Jews—who disobey the gospel (1 Pet 2:7–8).

In this book we have seen God's faithfulness to Israel mirrored through the life of Hosea, whose marriage partner had been unfaithful. Even so, in a move that reflected grace rather than law, God commanded him to take her back. At the end of Hosea, even after the prediction of a period of punishment for sin, the prophet announces that God is still willing to take Israel back and restore to her all the covenant blessings she had lost through disobedience. The eternal gospel could be foreshadowed in no greater way, for Christ "receives sinners", calls them to repentance, and grants them a privileged place among his people.

Suggested Further Reading

Peter C. Craigie, Twelve Prophets (London: Westminster John Knox, 1984)

J. Dearman, The Book of Hosea, NIV Commentary (Grand Rapids: Eerdmans, 2010)

Frederick Tatford, *Prophet of a Broken Home* (Eastbourne: Prophetic Witness, 1974)

Hans Walter Wolff, Hosea. Hermeneia: A Critical & Historical Commentary on the Bible (Minneapolis: Augsburg, 1974)

www.ingramcontent.com/pod-product-compliance
Lightning Source LLC
Chambersburg PA
CBHW060417090426
42734CB00011B/2345